The Baby Wait

Disclaimer

This book is designed to increase knowledge, awareness and understanding of fertility issues. It is not intended to replace the advice that your own doctor can give you. If you are concerned by any of the issues raised in this book make sure you consult your GP, who is there to help you.

Whilst every effort has been made to ensure the accuracy of the information and material contained in this book, nevertheless it is possible that errors or omissions may occur in the content. The author and publishers assume no responsibility for and give no guarantees or warranties concerning the accuracy, completeness or up-to-date nature of the information provided in this book.

The Baby Wait

Lessons Learned While Trying to Become a Mum

Lyn Sharkey

ORPEN PRESS

Published by
Orpen Press
Lonsdale House
Avoca Avenue
Blackrock
Co. Dublin
Ireland

e-mail: info@orpenpress.com
www.orpenpress.com

Paperback ISBN 978-1-871305-95-1
ePub ISBN 978-1-909518-42-1
Kindle ISBN 978-1-909518-43-8

Printed in Dublin by SPRINTprint Ltd.

This book is dedicated to Dessie.

Melody Cool
I've see a million bridges in my time and crossed every one of them
With no trouble at all
I've had trials and tribulations, heartaches and pains …
Survived 'em all baby

I'm *still* Melody
… and I'm still cool

Excerpt from 'Melody Cool' by Prince and the New Power Generation, *Grafitti Bridge*, Lead Vocals Mavis Staples (Paisley Park/Warner Bros, 1990)

Acknowledgements

Thank you so much to my wonderful husband, Dessie, who is the source of my love and laughter. I struck lucky when I was born into my fabulous family who have been unconditionally loving and totally supportive my whole life – Mum, Nikki, Emer, Annette, Brian, Maureen, Rachel, Brian Jnr, Fr Brian (*The Life of Brian* is also one of my favourite films) and also to Gaga (Brian the first and the man who always made me feel safe), Nana, Auntie Pat and Jim, who I know are all watching over us still.

Thank you to my friends, Finola, Josephine, Roisín, Corina, Fiona, Siobhan and Paula, for ignoring the taboo and having those fertility conversations with me. Thanks to Freda for her friendship and my all-American friend Colleen, who not only helped me with my diet but has been a great support too. Thanks to Marty for being a friend and making my sister so happy. Thanks to Peggy for her prayers and to Simon for his thoughtfulness. Thanks to my nieces and nephews for their love and fun. Thanks to my mother-in-law, Nuala, for her constant optimism that we will succeed.

Thank you to Ronnie and Dr Olga Turner for making me healthy again and changing the way I approached my fertility issues. Thank you to Teri Shanahan for helping me enormously with craniosacral therapy and for being a friend. Thank you to Ann, my 'hairdressapist' (our new word for hairdresser-cum-therapist), for setting the world to rights with me and introducing me to EFT. Thank you to Nicola Hamill and Heather Leeson (Positive Nutrition) for helping me with my diet. Thank you Caroline Dimascio for telling me about the book *Is Your Body Baby-Friendly?* and for the nutrition tips.

I have mentioned my most constant supporters and people who have actually changed the course of my thinking or my health, but there are many others who have been helpful and kind along the way. Thank you also to other relations and friends, medical professionals, therapists, colleagues and clients who may have offered sympathetic words, cups of tea or even just a wink or a squeeze of my arm to show they understood. You have all enriched my life and enabled me to feel absolutely blessed, despite our fertility problems. Thank you to the wonder of Google (I remember typewriters and word processors) for helping me to find legitimate studies and case histories online, and for providing the resource for me to find endless information on nutrition.

Finally, last but definitely not least, thank you so much to Orpen Press for publishing my book. I must mention Elizabeth Brennan and my editor, Eileen O'Brien, who took so much care to understand what needed to be said.

Contents

Contents

Contents

Preface

Hi, and thank you so much for picking up my little book. My name is Lyn, and my lovely husband, Dessie, and I have been trying to successfully carry a baby for nine years now. As I don't actually have a baby in my arms yet, I am sure that you are wondering what advice I can possibly offer. The thing is, I absolutely believe that if I knew at the beginning all that I know now we would have our baby already. A huge amount of our time has been wasted flailing in uncertainty, due to lack of diagnosis and lack of our own knowledge, so I feel compelled to ensure that this won't happen to you and hopefully save some of your precious time. It is my hope that I can pass on all that I have learned along the way and help you with some practical advice and friendly support. Although I am not a fertility expert, I am now an expert on my own fertility and I would urge you to become your own expert too.

We are really optimistic at the moment and have finally solved a lot of our problems (unfortunately it can happen that you have a combination of problems). It is actually only by a process of elimination that you discover what your issues are, so it is important to know what you need to eliminate. Of course, it would have been easier if I had gotten to this stage in my thirties but maybe if I have learned something along the way that will help someone else I can live with that. Everyone says that as soon as your baby arrives you forget all of the pain that went beforehand. I don't really want to forget. I want to try to do something to help relieve the stress and sometimes unbearable grief that thousands of women and men live with every day, unnoticed by the rest of the world. Even perfectly fertile couples can take up to a year to conceive and this can be confusing and stressful. I also hope that if more people comprehend what we go through then this subject won't be such a taboo in future.

When Dessie and I first decided that we were ready to start our family, I was totally naive and it did not even cross my mind that I wouldn't fall pregnant as soon as we wanted to. I have always been maternal and can actually remember the first time I felt that I seriously needed to have a baby. I was carrying a large bag of potatoes on my hip and realised that actually there was something else that belonged there. That might sound silly but it's absolutely true! Anyway, we didn't come home with the expected honeymoon baby and, after a few months, it began to slowly dawn on me that it wouldn't be as easy as I had thought. It was definitely a slow dawning because I just couldn't believe (and didn't really want to accept) that this was happening to us. We have since been through the mill in our quest to bring a little mini-me or mini-Dessie into the world. With hindsight, I can see that we knew so little about fertility in general and that so much time could have been saved if we had been better prepared and informed.

When you think about it, we are taught biology at school but not much about fertility. It doesn't occur to us that we need to know anything (apart from the obvious 'how to ...') because it will surely happen naturally once we are ready, as it does for millions of women all over the world every day. However, there are some simple things that we can do before we even start trying to conceive which will improve our general health and help us to better manage our stressful lifestyles, which arguably are contributing to increasing infertility statistics. Experts are forecasting that one in four couples will face challenges in conceiving within the next ten years. Wouldn't it be great if we could change that? I hope that you find the advice in Chapter 1 useful. You will already recognise some of the tips and some will be new, but I hope that my layman's explanations, combined with my own experience of how they helped me in the end, will encourage you to understand why they are necessary for everyone to consider. Our diets could be improved and our stress levels reduced, and this can only help to ensure healthier babies. I can assure you from my own experience that while they won't solve every fertility problem there is they will solve some of them and they will definitely save you invaluable time in the long run.

I know that once you are prepared, most of you will conceive quickly. However, it can sometimes take longer than you would wish. Trying to conceive and all of the emotions that are involved can be a frustrating experience at times, so I have also attempted to remember all of those questions I asked myself and all of those feelings I had along the way, so that readers who are feeling upset or stressed by the process can have this little book to dip into to get some answers and support. You are not losing your mind and you are not the only one who has gone through this endurance test.

It would be an absolute bonus if this book also helped to inform family, friends, doctors, nurses and therapists in some way about what their loved one or patient is going through. Being treated successfully by a doctor or therapist must be a two-way relationship. Speaking from a patient's point of view, it is easier to trust someone when they meet us halfway with some degree of understanding. For doctors and therapists, it is important that their patients are open and honest with them so they can treat them properly.

Infertility is a subject which is not really discussed comfortably for some reason. However, there is no reason why this should be the case, especially as fertility is such a huge and natural part of everyone's life. This reluctance only makes those of us suffering through infertility feel as though people think it is something to be ashamed of. We can make a change, however, by speaking openly on the topic and reducing these unnecessary stresses will certainly benefit us.

I sincerely hope that most of you won't need to read past Chapter 1 for yourselves, although reading the entire book will help you to understand what other women are living with.

I wish each of you lots and lots of love and joy in your life. Whatever happens along the way, don't forget to laugh every day (or as often as you can) and surround yourself with good people. Remember always that life is a gift and that means yours, and not just the little dote you are dreaming of holding in your arms.

Luv Lyn xxx

1

Preparing for Pregnancy

Mr Right

Before I begin, I would just like to pay tribute to my Mr Right, my Dessie. He is my secret weapon! He is my best friend and my hero. He is just the funniest person I have ever met and will go to any lengths to make me laugh. He looks after me when I need it, lets me look after him, gives me excellent advice and is always positively supportive. Because of his pure soul and gorgeous smile, I can say that, although we have had a tough time with regard to starting our family since we got married, we have also had wonderful times with lots of fun, and are happy. When I am beside him, wherever we are, even on my worst days, all is right with the world. Make sure you start your family with your Mr Right and you will get through all of the ups and downs that life throws at us with a smile on your face (most days).

The Three-Month Plan

So you want to have a baby. How wonderful! You are in a loving relationship and are ready to start your family. This is a great time and it makes you feel all warm and fuzzy at the very idea of it.

Now, if you were going to run a marathon, you would plan and train to make sure that your body was in shape for this physically demanding and gruelling exercise. When you think about it, pregnancy is something that none of us prepare for and we just all take for granted that it will go well for us. Pregnancy changes your body and your hormones, and the resulting child changes your life. If I could start all over again, I believe that a little preparation would go a long way and ensure that you both have the best possible start to your new life. Somebody said to me once, 'I didn't need to do all that stuff – I'm so fertile I can get pregnant when I want', and in my head I just said back 'Bully for you', while smiling back through gritted teeth. After all, even if you can get pregnant at the drop of a hat, being as fit and healthy as possible can only serve to increase your all-round quality and enjoyment of life and make your pregnancy easier and more enjoyable. You will need lots of stamina when the baby finally arrives too. During pregnancy, your baby is starting from scratch and laying the foundations for their future physical self so you will also be doing your utmost to ensure their long-term health and well-being. The following sections go through some simple, inexpensive and basic things that you could do in the three months before you start trying to conceive.

Charting Methods

Why Should We Chart?

We may think that we know our fertility or menstrual cycle because we know roughly how long it usually is, but it can be a different story when we record it over a few months. It is amazing how many women don't actually know their cycle or when they ovulate (when a mature egg is released from one or other ovary, ready for fertilisation), and therefore their fertile period, and are then so upset because they are not getting pregnant immediately. My sister Nikki and I recently carried out an ovulation study. Ten women charted their cycle over a period of six months using a product that we sell, called Maybe Baby, which is a re-usable saliva ovulation test. One of our participants had been trying to conceive a baby for over a year. Once she started charting her cycle, she conceived during her second cycle. Her cycle had possibly changed after her previous pregnancies and charting gave her the information she needed to conceive again. Another woman I was speaking to once was very upset after six months of trying unsuccessfully. She was really stressed but it turned out that she hadn't a clue about ovulation. Once I help her to understand her cycle and gave her some other little tips, she became pregnant very quickly. What I didn't realise for a long time was that our cycle can actually vary from month to month, depending on factors such as stress and illness. We don't all ovulate on Day 14–16 or even every month either. Ovulation can occur as early as Day 8 or as late as Day 22. I always had a regular-as-clockwork 28-day cycle, so it was presumed my ovulation was normal Day 14. However, when I started charting, I discovered that I wasn't ovulating until Day 19 or 20. This indicated that my luteal phase (from ovulation to menstruation) was too short, as it was only eight days and should be approximately fourteen. This in turn indicated that my progesterone was too low, which was later proven with a blood test.

Another myth that I would like to bust now is that you ovulate from the right ovary one month and the left the next and so on. Some women will be aware of which side they are ovulating from because they will get an ovulation pain or twinge; however, not everyone will experience this sensation. Unfortunately for us, I have one 'clubbed' fallopian tube due to endometriosis, which means that my left tube is closed, for all intents and purposes, and so it would not be possible for an egg to enter it. When I heard this, I presumed that this meant that my chances were reduced by 50 per cent, that I would only have an egg available for fertilisation every second month. However, I was advised by a nurse that, actually, your ovaries and fallopian tubes are not connected. There is a type of magnetic field that pulls the egg into the fallopian tube once it has been released from the ovary. So even if I ovulate from my left side (the damaged tube side) there is a small possibility that my right tube will pull it in. There is also the possibility that I will ovulate from my right ovary more often. Of course, unless I have ultrasound follicle tracking scans every month, we can't be sure exactly what the actual chances are in percentage terms but I prefer to be positive and believe every month is an opportunity. As individuals, we are more than statistical chances anyway.

Knowing precisely when you are in your fertile period is vital information to help maximise your chances of conceiving as quickly as possible and also in case you need to have blood tests on certain days. In fact, the couple of days before ovulation are the best days to try to conceive. Start charting your cycle now. I wish I had thought of doing this in my twenties even before I was ready to have children so that I would know if and when my cycle changed. I believe that charting for a couple of months every year, even if you never want to have babies, would be a sensible thing for every woman to do. Our fertility is obviously directly related to our general wellness and any changes can indicate that we need to pay attention to our health. There are several ways to do this and you can use a combination if you like, to be sure.

Saliva Ovulation Test

My fertility learning curve only really began when I started charting my cycle about three years ago. Saliva ovulation tests are based on the fact that when oestrogen is present in dried saliva a fern-like pattern crystallizes and this can be seen clearly through a microscope. Oestrogen is the first hormone to increase when you are coming into your fertile period. It prepares the body for ovulation and makes the womb welcoming to sperm as it instigates the production of cervical mucus, which protects the sperm and helps it along its journey into the fallopian tubes. On non-fertile days you will see a 'pebbles and dots' pattern. When this oestrogen surge first happens, you will see a transition pattern, which is a mixture of pebbles and dots and some ferning and can happen from between two and four days before ovulation. This is the signal to start trying to conceive as these few days before ovulation are the best days to try. At the time of ovulation, the fern pattern will be at its most dense. Monitoring this hormone surge gives you your first indication that ovulation is imminent. Because the test is re-usable, the mini microscope can be used every single day to chart your cycle.

By the way, I have to declare my interest here. My sister Nikki and I were using one particular type of test – the Maybe Baby re-usable saliva ovulation tester – for a while and absolutely loved it; so much so that we put our money where our mouth is and became distributors for Ireland and the UK. It is a clean and user-friendly ovulation test, with a six-month chart included in each unit. It is also cost effective as it is completely re-usable and will only need to have a battery replaced eventually. To use it you simply lick the underside of the microscope to deposit a saliva sample, leave to dry for 10–15 minutes and then examine the pattern formed and record it on your chart. You then just wipe the microscope clean before your next test with the lint cloth provided. Your chart gives you the following useful information (see my chart on the facing page):

- Regularity and length of your cycle
- Regularity and timing of ovulation (can occur as early as Day 8 or as late as Day 22 and may not be on the same day every month)
- If ovulation occurs at all (some months you might not ovulate due to stress or illness)
- If you ovulate twice in a cycle (some research suggests that this may happen due to lunar influences)
- Length of your luteal phase (from ovulation to menstruation should be approximately fourteen days; if this is too short, it can indicate lower levels of progesterone)
- Your transitional pattern will let you know that you are about to ovulate and this is the time to start trying

You should also note on your chart if you have had a particularly stressful day or have been ill, and you can then see the impact of these events on your ovulation patterns. If you can see that stress is affecting your fertility that will provide motivation to take steps to reduce or better manage stress in your life.

Should you need to see a doctor at some stage, your chart history will provide very useful information and if you require blood tests it will ensure that you have them at the right point in your cycle.

Opposite is an example of my chart, which illustrates a short luteal phase and indicates low progesterone levels.

DAY	Month 1	Month 2	Month 3	Month 4	Month 5	Month 6	EXAMPLE
1	M	M	M	M	M	M	M
2	M	M	M	M	M	M	M
3	M	M	M	M	M	M	M
4	M	M	M	M	M	M	M
5	M	M	M	M	M	M	-
6	M	M	M	M	M	M	-
7	-	-	-	-	-	-	-
8	-	-	-	-	-	-	-
9	-	-	-	-	-	-	-
10	-	-	-	-	-	-	-
11	-	-	-	-	-	-	T
12	-	-	-	-	-	-	T
13	-	-	-	-	-	-	T
14	-	-	-	-	-	-	O
15	-	-	-	-	-	-	O
16	-	-	T	-	T	-	T
17	T	-	T	-	T	T	T
18	T	T	T	T	-	T	T
19	O	T	O	T	-	O	-
20	-	O	-	O	-	-	-
21	-	-	-	-	-	-	-
22	-	-	-	-	-	-	-
23	-	-	-	-	-	-	-
24	-	-	-	-	-	-	-
25	-	-	-	-	-	-	-
26	-	-	-	-	-	-	-
27	-	-	-	-	-	-	-
28		-		-			-
29							
30							
31							

Key to chart: M = Menstruation, – = Not Fertile, T = Transition Phase, O = Ovulation

Mid-Stream or Urine Ovulation Tests

Luteinizing hormone (LH) is a hormone released by the pituitary gland in the brain. Increasing levels of this hormone in women causes ovulation to occur, i.e. the release of the egg from the follicle, which is a fluid-filled sac in which the immature egg develops. Urine tests let you know when this surge occurs, indicating your fertile period. Like a pregnancy test, this test involves urinating onto a stick or placing the stick in a sterile container of urine. If a sufficient quantity of LH is present in your urine the test will change to a specific colour or indicate a positive sign. They are accurate, of course, but I believe they should be used in conjunction with other charting methods, because most women use these tests for one week of their cycle only. I believe that you really need to be charting every single day of your cycle so that you can see the patterns of your whole cycle and don't miss ovulation in cases where you ovulate earlier or later than usual.

Cervical Mucus Monitoring

Cervical mucus is exactly what it says: mucus produced by your cervix. In the past, you may have never even noticed it. However, it is there and if you start to check it you will notice that it changes in quality throughout your cycle. You can check your cervical mucus by wiping yourself with tissue paper, and then using your clean fingers to check the consistency and stretchability of the mucus. During ovulation, it should be clear or opaque and stretch more than an inch. Wet and slippery mucus is what you are looking for at the time of ovulation. Sperm have to travel through this mucus to get to the egg, which is why the quality of it is so important. It also provides nourishment to enable sperm to live for up to five days after ejaculation. However, everyone is different and some women will produce more than others. For some women, the change is not very obvious and this is why it is so important to take the time to learn the individual signals your own body gives you – they might not be the same as someone else's but this doesn't necessarily mean that there is a problem.

It can take time to learn how to read the signs of the changes in your cervical mucus so don't panic, but it is a completely free way of checking your fertility. You can use it in addition to other methods to help keep track of your cycle. If you are interested in this method there is a book by Toni Weschler called *Taking Charge of Your Fertility* which takes you through this method of charting, and also the basal temperature charting method, in very great detail.

Basal Temperature Charting

Your basal temperature means your 'at-rest' temperature. This charting method involves taking your temperature as soon as you wake up each morning and before you even move to get up. This method will only tell you that ovulation has occurred after it has occurred. It is based on the fact that your 'at rest' body temperature will drop a wee bit before ovulation and then rise by 0.5 degrees Celsius after ovulation has occurred. It remains raised until your period arrives, when it will drop again.

As the days *before* ovulation are the most fertile, this is not the most useful method to use when trying to conceive, but if you use it to chart your cycle over a period of months you can determine how regular it is. However, you must remember that other factors can affect your temperature, for example illness and alcohol, so it is not always a reliable indicator. In my opinion, this method is used ideally to back up your other fertility observations.

Visit a Nutritionist

No matter how many times we hear that proper nutrition is essential for a healthy pregnancy it bears repeating because it is so vitally important and yet not everyone wants to consider changing their eating habits. A healthy balanced diet is, of course, the best way to get the nutrients we need for good health. However, a healthy diet for you is possibly not the same as a healthy diet for me and this is why we need to be aware of what our bodies are telling us. I would really recommend that everyone visit a dietician or nutritionist to get some individually tailored advice and to check for food allergies and intolerances at this stage. Be aware that not every doctor places as much emphasis on food intolerances and some will tell you to just eat a balanced diet as per the food pyramid. When choosing a dietician or nutritionist choose carefully, using word of mouth or choosing one who is affiliated with a professional organisation such as the Irish Nutrition and Dietetic Institute, the Irish section of the Nutrition Society or the Irish Institute of Nutrition and Health.

Please take this one seriously. Food intolerances are a huge part of my story and while I know that I am an extreme case, I am also aware that there is a high incidence of wheat and dairy intolerance in this part of the world and as these can impact directly on your fertility it really is worth checking out. I know this from experience, from both the improved results of my bloods tests and how I felt so much better once I cut out certain foods.

I always thought I could eat anything, as food never made me feel ill or nauseous, which is what you would expect food intolerances to do. However, ever since I was a teenager, I have had to take iron supplements and tonics for anaemia. I put my fatigue down to being very busy and the fact that everyone complains about being tired these days. Looking back I didn't even realise quite how tired I was. My mum noticed that if I called in the morning I was great but after lunch I would be yawning a lot. I would always be wrecked after eating a large meal as well even though, when you think about it, food is our fuel so really you should feel energised after eating. I was advised to cut out gluten because despite my nutritious diet I had no iron or vitamins to speak of in my blood. I started to feel better within a few weeks of starting my gluten-free diet and was happily keeping to it because I had so much more energy. However, I had another food intolerance test carried out through a laboratory in the UK and my updated list of intolerances included dairy, egg whites, soya, wheat, barley, rye, nuts, pasta, rice, corn, maize, potatoes (What? A good Irish cailín not being able to eat spuds?!), broccoli, cabbage, oranges, lemons, pears ... – is that enough for you? Even the people in the laboratory that carried out the test were not used to seeing such a long list. The fact that I got run down so much can actually be a symptom of coeliac disease. It is fairly obvious, however, that my body's reaction to food was an indicator that there was something wrong with my immune system, which my fertility issues are also related to. It was not an easy job to establish a new diet for myself which satisfied all of usual dietary requirements but, after lots of research, I did. I bawled like a little baby several times while trying to figure out how I was going to feed my hungry self, but I had to because my immune system was reacting so strongly to the food I ate that antibodies were being created in my blood which fought off anything and everything that was considered a foreign body. As you can imagine, this was unfortunately not very conducive to maintaining a healthy pregnancy.

Admittedly, it is a total pain in the neck when you change your diet in the beginning, especially because people don't always understand why you are being so 'picky'. You can't exactly explain to most people that you are terrified you might miscarry because they will just think you are ridiculous. The link between food intolerance and fertility is a new concept for many people. Thankfully, there are lots of alternative foods out there now and when you start to feel healthy and vital again it is so worth the trouble. I take oat milk instead of cows' milk, make ice-cream with coconut cream, use buckwheat flakes or gluten-free oats instead of cereal, and eat quinoa, which I talk about below, along with some other superfoods which ensure I get all of the vitamins and minerals I need. This dietary journey has also totally changed how I think about food and my tastes have changed accordingly. I visited a couple of nutritionists and researched on the internet to develop my current healthy diet. However, mine was a very extreme case so don't panic or worry if you have a minor allergy to strawberries or something like that. It is just sensible to check it out now and avoid any foods that are not suitable for you, saving time and energy later.

If you find that you have no food intolerances, then fantastic. Stick with a varied and balanced diet with lots of fruit and particularly vegetables, as much organic food as possible and as little sugar as possible. However, if you find that you have intolerances, please take them seriously as they can also inhibit your absorption of nutrients from food, so you won't have any to pass on to your baby and you will become fatigued and run down. You will also reduce the risk of passing your allergies or intolerances on to your little one. I actually think that this is something that everyone should do for the sake of their own health and vitality. Our physiologies are all individual and you wouldn't put diesel into a petrol car would you? A simple change of diet can enhance your quality of life enormously so that you are really living and enjoying your life and not just dragging yourself through your day.

If you are interested in learning more, a good book to read on this subject is Patrick Holford's *Optimum Nutrition Before, During and After Pregnancy*. It details good diets but, of course, it can't cater for all allergies and intolerances so you may need to tailor some of the advice to suit yourself. Your local health food shop should be able to recommend a good dietician or nutritionist and can often give you excellent tips for your new diet. Your dietician or nutritionist may also be able to check for toxins and yeast in your system and advise you on how to clear them. By the way, eating healthily will also help you to avoid the complication of gestational diabetes, another increasingly common issue that mums-to-be are facing.

Vitamins, Minerals and Supplements

In an ideal world, we would all eat purely organic food and get all of our nutrients from this natural source. However, it is not always possible to source all of our food from organic suppliers. Modern-day diets and living can mean that we need to supplement our diet with vitamin and mineral preparations, and this is particularly true when preparing to conceive.

We all know that we should take folic acid for three months before we even start trying to get pregnant. However, there are other vitamins and minerals which are also essential for a healthy baby and which we may not be getting from our diet. You can get a good conception supplement from your pharmacy or health food shop, which will include most of these together with your folic acid. Pregnacare Conception and Marilyn Glenville's Fertility for Women are two good ones, and are widely available. There are also conception supplements for your partner, like Wellman Conception, and he should take these up to conception also. It is also a good idea to take omega-3 if you don't eat enough oily fish and calcium if you are dairy intolerant. Just make sure that if you buy a fish oil supplement for omega-3 it doesn't contain Vitamin A, as you should not supplement this vitamin once you get pregnant. High doses of Vitamin A during pregnancy can lead to birth defects and liver toxicity. For this reason you should always ensure any supplements you are taking are suitable for use during pregnancy and not double up on supplements. However, you should double check any supplements you wish to take with your doctor or dietician/nutritionist to ensure it suits your individual needs, especially if you have any underlying health issues. For example, if you have haemachromatosis, which is quite common in Celtic people, then your body produces too much iron and so you definitely should not supplement iron or Vitamin C, which aids iron absorption.

To understand why these vitamins and minerals are so important, in case you need persuading, these are the reasons why they are vital for you now:

- *Folic Acid* – Folic acid is taken to prevent spina bifida in your future baby and recent studies are showing that it can help to prevent cleft palates also. It is very important to take folic acid before becoming pregnant and throughout pregnancy to ensure you have adequate levels.
- *Vitamin B Complex* – Taking Vitamin B12 and all the other B vitamins is important to ensure that your body metabolises protein, fats and carbohydrates. It also helps form new red blood cells, antibodies and neurotransmitters, and is vital to your baby's developing brain and nervous system.
- *Calcium* – It is vital to build up your calcium stores before trying to conceive so that when you are pregnant you will have plenty for both you and your baby, and so your teeth will stay healthy. When you become

pregnant, your developing baby will need calcium to build strong bones and teeth, and to grow a healthy heart, nerves and muscles. If you don't get enough calcium in your diet when you are pregnant, your baby will draw it from your bones, which may impair your own health later on. You should be getting your calcium supply from the food you eat if possible; the best sources for calcium are superfoods (see below), dairy products (which are easily absorbed), dark leafy greens, almonds and sesame seeds. If you are intolerant of dairy products there are substitutes like coconut, soya and oat milk. Oat milk is my favourite as it tastes quite like cows' milk but is a little sweeter (once you get over the beige colour and make sure you shake the carton before pouring). I try to get my daily calcium from my food, namely oat milk, sesame seeds and vegetables. However, because I can't take dairy products and osteoporosis is in my family, I also take supplemental calcium, magnesium and Vitamin D (which helps the body to absorb calcium).

- *Zinc* – Zinc is a mineral that is essential for fertility in both men and women, but especially for men as it is involved in building good sperm, and is important for healthy testicles and an increased sperm count. It has to be constantly replaced as it is lost in every ejaculation. Foods rich in zinc include lean meats, beans, Brazil nuts and sesame seeds.
- *Vitamin C* – Vitamin C is important for women because it ensures you have healthy hormone levels, increases fertility, keeps the immune system healthy and aids the absorption of iron. However, too much Vitamin C can create an acidic environment in the vagina and dry up cervical fluid so make sure you stick to the recommended dosage. For men, Vitamin C is helpful in keeping sperm from clumping and improves their movement. Great food

sources of Vitamin C are red bell peppers, oranges and strawberries.

- *Vitamin E* – Vitamin E is very important for the reproductive system of both men and women. For women, it is essential for maintaining the endocrine system and the absorption of essential fatty acids, which are used to produce hormones. For men, Vitamin E aids in producing sperm and key sex hormones, and protects sperm from mutation. The best sources of Vitamin E are watercress, dark leafy greens, liver, sunflower oil, pumpkin seeds and wheat germ.
- *Iron* – Iron is a blood-building nutrient that improves fertility by helping to balance ovulation. The best form of iron is from a whole food supplement. Sources of iron include lean red meat – including beef, lamb and pork – liver, tuna (once a week only), shrimp, salmon, kidney beans, lentils, spinach, kale, broccoli and tofu.
- *L-Arginine* – L-Arginine is an amino acid which increases the blood flow to the reproductive system. It enhances libido, increases cervical mucus, ensures a healthy environment for implantation and may extend fertility for women over 40. The research behind this information was a major scientific breakthrough and actually won a Nobel Prize for Physiology and Medicine.
- *Essential Fatty Acids* – EFAs (including omega-3) are essential for the production of hormones in both women and men. Hormones use these fats as building blocks for what will become progesterone and many other reproductive hormones. Docosahexaenoic acid (DHA) is an EFA that helps with the formation of the brain in utero. The best sources of DHA are sea vegetables. I have looked up 'sea vegetables' and it includes many things I have never heard of. However, two familiar items were

seaweed and kelp. They are generally available from health food shops.

- *Selenium* — Selenium protects against cell mutation and helps to prevent cellular damage from free radicals. This is a trace mineral and so only needed in small amounts. Selenium can be found in nuts, cereals, meat, mushrooms, fish, eggs, sunflower seeds, liver and bran.

Choline and Betaine

Choline and betaine are not really talked about enough with regard to fertility and may not be included in your conception supplement. Choline has only recently been added to the Vitamin B family and is important for fertility. Choline can help prevent fatty build-up in the liver. Research has shown that choline is found not only in the pancreas and liver but is also, in fact, a component of every human cell. It is great for the brain development of your baby and too little can impact on learning abilities. Experts now say that dietary choline intake is also particularly important during pregnancy as this nutrient, similar to folic acid, is needed for the proper formation of the brain and spinal column (see www.supplementalscience.com). Both choline and betaine supplements have also been reported to be of value in helping prevent cardiovascular disease. This alone should be enough to make anyone pay attention to their choline and betaine intakes. Choline is best absorbed from your diet, particularly egg yolks, cauliflower, soya bean products (lecithin) and, to a lesser degree, oats, lentils, butter, peanuts and peanut butter, potatoes, tomatoes, bananas, milk, oranges, barley, corn, sesame seeds, flax seeds and wholemeal bread.

Betaine helps our body to properly absorb and utilise choline, so it is important that you also get enough betaine in your diet, though spinach, beetroot, grains and shellfish. The best way to ensure your choline and betaine intake (and so the proper development of your baby's brain and spinal column) is sufficient is to include some or all of the above healthy foods in your shopping trolley, especially eggs, cauliflower, spinach and beetroot.

Tea, Coffee, Green Tea and Herbal Tea

The general consensus seems to be that you should limit your caffeine intake for good health. Caffeine causes blood vessels to constrict and so can reduce blood flow (this includes blood flow to the placenta when you are pregnant, which can impact on the baby's developing cells). I have found no studies that say you need to cut caffeine out altogether, but definitely cut down if you drink a lot of it. I used to love a cappuccino when I met my friends for coffee but I never felt that great afterwards, funnily enough. It wasn't that hard for me to give up coffee, but I know some people do find it difficult.

There are some really good brands of decaffeinated tea and coffee available which taste exactly the same as 'ordinary' tea and coffee. I also used to drink an awful lot of green tea, which is a terrific source of antioxidants, to boost my immune system. However, while this tea has beneficial properties it still contains caffeine and so is not good to drink during the second half of your cycle if you are trying to conceive. This last fact was difficult for me to hear as I drank so much green tea for a couple of years that the thought of it being harmful to my chances of getting pregnant was hard to deal with. Reasonably, my brain knew that I had bigger issues to contend with and I am sure that a doctor would laugh if I blamed my problems on too much green tea. However, once I had heard it I wished I had known this fact at the beginning so that I would never have to wonder if I had unwittingly been contributing to my fertility problems. This is one of the reasons why I wanted to write down every little and big thing that I ever learned, so that you could know from the beginning and never have to grieve for time wasted through not knowing. Anyway, you live and learn, and move forward; I have now switched to chamomile and other berry teas, with a few cups of green tea in the first half of my cycle only. I really like herbal teas but I know some people who can't take to them at all. However, even if you cut down on your caffeine and switch every second cup to decaffeinated or herbal tea (or 'horrible tea' as Dessie calls it) this can only benefit your health. You should also remember that some soft drinks and energy drinks, such as Coca-Cola, Pepsi and Red Bull, also contain caffeine.

Detox

Doing a detox at least once a year is a great idea for all of us, whether we are trying to conceive or not. I could scare the living daylights out of you with all of the facts and figures about what toxins we live with in our environment but there is no point in worrying about things that are outside of our control. So I would rather take up your time by telling you about the positive things you can do to counteract the effects of these toxins. We all know that the air we breathe and the food we eat can contain things that are bad for us, such as exhaust fumes and pesticides. The physical effect of this is that our poor livers and kidneys are working overtime to deal with the offending and unnatural substances that need to be eliminated from our systems.

So what can we do to help support the function of these organs and keep ourselves clean inside? There are many detox programmes available through your local health food shop.

All of them have the same aim – to help the body to eliminate toxins from your system. You must ensure that you detox healthily and this does not mean starving yourself or sticking to one type of food for a week. Your local health food shop will recommend a detox to suit your individual requirements. This can be in the form of taking a simple herbal tea and drinking lots of water. No matter what detox programme you follow, drinking lots of water is always a great way to help your body to eliminate toxins. You will get the most benefit from your detox by cutting out as much sugar as possible from your diet and all alcohol while you are detoxing. It couldn't be simpler. Not only will this remove the toxins from your system and so be great for your skin, but it will also relieve the pressure on your liver and kidneys so that they can work at their optimum level, which in turn means that the rest of your organs are less sluggish and so boost your energy levels. If there is a chance that you have yeast in your body (which is a high possibility given the amount of sugar in our diets), then a detox can help this also. Don't, however, detox if you are already pregnant, as some detox programmes may use herbs which may be harmful during pregnancy.

Another wee tip with regard to detoxing is to add coriander to your diet. Believe it or not, this lovely herb will help to carry metals out of your system. I had always thought that herbs were primarily added to dishes for aesthetic reasons, to make them look pretty. However, further to all of my research into nutrition I have discovered that they all have amazing health benefits. I add coriander to Thai curries and always to my soups (carrot, butternut squash and sweet potato soup especially; always add lentils to your soups as well because they not only bulk them up but are fabulously beneficial to your health and help to balance your blood sugars, so keeping you full for ages). See also the next section on superfoods as mung beans, chlorella and spirulina are brilliant for helping your system detox and function properly. Detoxing also helps your immune system enormously, which in turn keeps you healthy and disease free.

Finally, you may not realise but we detox every night while we are sleeping and the results of this can be seen on our tongue when we wake up. Did you know that your tongue can actually tell you a lot about the state of your organs? If you notice a film on your tongue in the mornings, these released toxins can be removed by simple scraping with a metal spoon or metal tongue scraper. Using a sweeping motion from as far back as possible to the front, scrape your tongue gently up to ten times, as soon as you get up. Ayurvedic medicine (Ayurveda) states that tongue scraping also stimulates your heart, lungs, kidneys, stomach, pancreas, intestine and colon. In addition, gently stimulating all of these organs helps to boost your immune system. Ladies, you must realise also that while we can apply all of the lotions and potions we want onto our skin, looking after our internal organs is the best way to prevent ageing too quickly and improve our outer appearance. Many acupuncturists study the tongue and if you visit one you could ask them to analyse yours. I recommend reading a book called *Ayurvedic Tongue Diagnosis* by Walter Shantree Kacera if you are interested in finding out more.

Superfoods for Health and Fertility

During my research I have come across some superfoods which have excited me so I am always eager to encourage others to try them. I have replaced supplements with a healthy diet, which includes the following superfoods, and I feel more vital than ever. As far as I am concerned, my overall health is important for two reasons. Being physically as well as possible really has helped me to cope with stress more easily and I feel very balanced and happy. My fertility issues are autoimmune disorders and so boosting my immune system and having a balanced system helps to improve these conditions. The proof is not only in how I feel but my blood tests are perfect these days, which is fantastic when you remember that I have been anaemic since I was a teenager. Maca root, açai berry, spirulina and chlorella are available in powder or tablet form. I prefer the powder because apart from the fact that it seems to be more cost effective and easier to absorb, I have a bad history of nearly choking on tablets – Dessie has banned me from taking any when I am alone in case the Heimlich manoeuvre is required. However, the powder form isn't to everyone's taste and so of course the tablets are great too. Boosting your overall health is the first thing that you should both do to increase your fertility. As with everything, if you have any underlying health issues you should check with your doctor when you consider taking supplements.

Maca Root

Maca root is a superfood which I came across for the first time last year by accident. The reviews of it are amazing so I have started to take it myself. When I started taking it at first, I got a huge boost in energy levels. Then my energy settled and I noticed that after two months, my luteal phase (from ovulation to menstruation) was lengthening and instead of my average eight days, it became eleven or twelve days long, which indicated that my progesterone levels were improved. I also noticed that my nails were stronger. I generally just feel better when maca root is part of my diet. Maca (known widely as Peruvian ginseng) is a root which has been used in the Peruvian Andes as a source of nourishment and healing for thousands of years. The story goes that back in the day, when the Spanish Conquistadors invaded South America and settled with their families and livestock in the Andes, they began to experience fertility problems (multiple miscarriages and difficulty conceiving) and their livestock also stopped reproducing, probably due to the change in altitude. They noticed that the locals were fine and eventually began to eat maca root, which was a staple part of the indigenous diet for both people and animals. This solved their problems. (Wow – how come I am only finding this out now?) I'm not saying it will solve every problem, but it obviously helps a lot.

Maca root provides energy, balance and vitality. You can buy it in powder or capsule form and the powder form is actually not expensive (approximately €15 for 500g, which will last you a few months). If your local health food shop doesn't stock it you can buy it online (just make sure to buy a good organic brand). While it is good for overall health, it appears to be really beneficial for the endocrine system, which in turn supports fertility. I have come across studies by Dr Gloria Chacon de Popovici which have identified that there are four alkaloids present in maca root which nourish the endocrine system. A healthy endocrine system is absolutely vital in order to conceive. The endocrine system is made up of all of the glands that produce and secrete your hormones. Maca root is what they call an adaptogen, in that it works in the parts of the body that need it most. It can boost libido and combat fatigue. Maca root contains plant sterols, vitamins, essential minerals, and fatty and amino acids. If you buy the powder form, you can add it to water, cereals, smoothies or yoghurts. Start with a small dose (1/4 teaspoon) and work your way up to full teaspoon a day over a couple of weeks. Of course, you should watch out for any individual side effects you might have, as with everything. If you are on any medication for underlying health issues it is always wise to discuss supplements with your doctor. You should check reviews and studies for yourself on the internet but it seems to me to be a no brainer that this superfood should be on your list of things to consider when you are preparing for pregnancy, particularly if your blood tests results show any hormone imbalances. www. irelandsrawkitchen.ie, www.andeanharvest.com and www. menstruation.com.au are three websites to start your research.

I was on fertility medication for over a year and in the middle of that had surgery. The medication was tough and post-operation I experienced side effects that were not conducive to conception. It was a big decision to make but I eventually decided to come off everything to get myself healthy again and, as part of the regime that I worked out for myself, started taking maca root powder. As I mentioned earlier, I am glad to say that my cycle and health have both returned to better than normal and I love this superfood. It is also supposed to be helpful for relieving the symptoms of menopause and studies have shown some success with increasing bone density in patients with osteoporosis.

Açaí Berry

Açaí (pronounced 'ah-sigh-ee') berry is becoming better known recently and is a fantastic superfood with many health benefits, particularly benefiting the immune system. It is claimed that açaí berry helps flush waste and toxins from your system, increases energy levels, boosts your metabolism, improves blood flow (improved circulation makes you feel better and live longer, and also improves mental clarity), improves your skin and helps it to look younger for longer, is great for the heart, helps reduce cholesterol, and contains antioxidants that work to eliminate harmful substances and so helps your immune system.

However, the better known açaí berry becomes, the more products appear on our shelves claiming to contain it and they may not have a high enough concentration to be really helpful. I would recommend taking açaí berry in either powder or juice form from reliable sources. Your local health food shop is always the best place to find recommended and trustworthy brands.

Chlorella

Chlorella is another excellent superfood (with a capital SUPER) to boost your immunity and promote overall health. It is actually a type of algae and nature's highest source of chlorophyll so is one of our primary superfoods. Due to its photosynthetic efficiency, it yields more protein per volume that any other plant. It is a source of carotenoids (antioxidants that neutralise harmful free radicals), B complex vitamins, Vitamins A, C and K, folic acid and polyunsaturated fat. Chlorella is also rich in nucleic acids, which are essential for cell regeneration in the body. I believe that overall health is essential for fertility. Fertility issues may be related to imbalances in other parts of our bodies, for example my issues are all related to my immune system. There are also studies which show that chlorella can increase blood levels of albumin, which is an essential protein that helps flush out toxins and heavy metals from your system. Chlorella is commonly used to balance pH levels in the body and it is claimed that it can boost the immune system, reduce high blood pressure, lower cholesterol levels and support friendly bacterial growth in the gut, improving digestion and bowel function. I would always recommend asking your local health food shop for advice on which products are from the most trustworthy sources also.

Spirulina

Spirulina, also a type of algae, is a blue/green powerhouse of protein, according to Ireland's Raw Kitchen (www.irelands rawkitchen.ie). It is brimful of B complex vitamins as well as Vitamins A, C, D and E, potassium, iron, calcium, magnesium, phosphorous, selenium, copper, zinc manganese, chromium and other trace minerals. It is rich in chlorophyll and phyco-cyanin and was used as a food source by the Aztecs of Central America.

There is a book available called *Superfoods for Optimum Health: Chlorella and Spirulina* by Mike Adams (a holistic health investigative journalist), which goes into great detail about the potential health benefits of these two superfoods. Apart from overall health benefits, there have been clinical studies carried out which claim that chlorella and spirulina can help prevent and contribute to curing all sorts of cancers, due to their cell regeneration and antioxidant properties.

As both spirulina and chlorella contain Vitamin A, I have been researching whether the levels in the recommended daily dosage are safe to take when you get pregnant. I have not found anything that says they are, although some say that there is not enough information to know for sure. Unfortunately there does not appear to be enough information to give a definitive answer to this question. As always, it is a good idea to consult with your doctor about any queries you have. If you are interested in taking these superfoods, it might be a good idea to take them up until you start trying to conceive and then check with your doctor and health food shop for more information. If in any doubt, you could stick with the conception supplements while you are trying.

Illness prevention is better than cure. You can get all of the above superfoods from your local health food shop or online. Two websites that I am familiar with which have good quality organic products are www.irelandsrawkitchen.com and www.thehappypear.ie.

Quinoa

Quinoa (pronounced 'keen-wah') is from South America and is also considered to be a superfood. Apparently, Incan warriors used to survive for days on this food alone. It contains the most complete protein of any grain and is gluten free, packed full of antioxidants and phytonutrients (natural chemicals found in a variety of plant foods), and can help to balance your blood sugar levels. Although it is classed as a grain it is actually a seed. It contains nine amino acids which are required by our bodies as building blocks for muscles (that's what 'complete protein' means). Quinoa also contains magnesium, which can help to reduce high blood pressure; fibre; and manganese and copper, which are antioxidants (compounds that many people believe can help to eliminate cancer and disease-causing substances from the body). I started eating it because it was a gluten-free option and I was just trying to fill myself up. I love it now and even more so since I realised just how healthy it is.

It is very easy to cook and as not all packages tell you how to cook it, I will now. Take one cup of quinoa and put it into a saucepan over heat. Toast the grains for a minute or two until you can smell the lovely aroma and then add two cups of water. Bring it to the boil and stir occasionally. The quinoa will have absorbed the water within about eight minutes and it's done. I always add a teaspoon of turmeric as well because this spice has anti-inflammatory properties (good for my endometriosis) and it turns it a lovely sunny yellow colour. The cooked quinoa is good mixed with roasted vegetables or cold with salad. It is great for absorbing any juices from tomatoes and cucumbers too so your lunch is never limp or soggy. Like couscous, quinoa adapts well to a wide variety of flavours, so it can be prepared with a variety of stocks, seasonings and spices to create many different dishes. You can find quinoa in all health food shops and some supermarkets in the health food section.

I also mix mung beans and sesame seeds with it, which add to the texture, while the sesame seeds provide a good source of calcium, manganese, copper, magnesium, iron, phosphorus, Vitamin B1, zinc and dietary fibre. By the way, sesame seeds belong to a group of fibres called lignans, which have been shown to reduce cholesterol levels, lower blood pressure and help reduce the risk factors for liver disease. Who knew these little seeds were so good for you?

Mung Beans

Mung beans are a legume and a great source of potassium needed for strong cardiovascular function and a healthy nervous system. They also contain fibre needed for the removal of excess cholesterol and old hormones from the body. Their fibre content also makes them great for blood sugar control as it slows down the release of sugars from carbohydrates.

Mung beans contain good levels of the B vitamins needed for the release of energy from food, including folic acid, needed for foetal development and cardiovascular health. When sprouted they develop good amounts of Vitamin C, needed by the immune system for healing and fending off infections.

Consumption of legumes such as mung beans has been strongly associated with a reduced risk of heart disease and healthy cholesterol levels. The magnesium and Vitamin B content also helps combat the effects of stress. Mung beans are good for detoxing as the fibre in them helps improve bowel function and they also absorb toxic residue from the sides of the intestinal walls.

Mung beans are very easy to cook and can be added to soups, stews and salads; they can be bought from your local health food shop and some supermarkets.

Bee Pollen

Bee pollen has a unique combination of minerals, vitamins, amino acids and enzymes and is especially potent in boosting your immune system if you take it from bees which are local to where you live. Your local health food shop would usually be a good place to source this.

Bee pollen has been used throughout history to restore energy and recuperative powers to ill people. It is believed to improve allergies in many people and hence may have a regulating effect on the immune system by helping to dampen unnecessary autoimmune attacks.

I keep a packet of bee pollen in the fridge and while I find it difficult to take on its own as it has a very strong taste, I add it to bars that I make at home with seeds and dried fruit. I have also added it to homemade ice cream, smoothies and cakes in small quantities. Even if you don't like the taste of something that is good for you, there are ways of including it in your diet. However, it is not recommended that bee pollen be taken while pregnant.

In this section, I really wanted to let people know about the foods that I have used because I believe that they are amazing and, apart from optimising fertility, I think that everyone should be aware of ways of keeping healthy and avoiding illness and disease. However, I also know that we all have different physiologies and so what works for me is not necessarily the answer for you. You really need to research everything and come up with a combination of nutrition, supplements and superfoods to suit your individual needs and take into account any underlying health issues that you might have, which you should always discuss with your doctor. A couple of good websites to use to start your research are www.whfoods.com and www.bodyecology.com.

Exercise

Regular gentle exercise – walking, swimming and gentle yoga – is fantastic at helping you de-stress and keeps the blood flowing. Flowing blood brings much-needed oxygen to every cell in your body and exercise releases happy endorphins. Pick a gentle exercise that you enjoy and then you will keep it up. Regular exercise is also a key component of keeping fit and healthy, which will improve your chances of conceiving. Enough said! However, if you are not used to vigorous exercise, gentle is the key word.

Stress

Stress can play a huge part in causing fertility issues for both men and women. It depletes the body of essential nutrients and has an impact on every area of your life. There are so many ways of dealing with stress. Pick one that you are attracted to and focus on it. I have several tools that I have used at different times. A good walk in the fresh air definitely helps. I like meditation and emotional freedom techniques (EFT), which is a cousin to acupuncture but without needles. It involves tapping on various acupressure points and you can learn to do it on yourself. See www.emofree.com for more information. I have actually done one of Gary Craig's courses on EFT and I found it helped friends and family with migraine, any type of headache, arthritis pain and anxiety. It is so simple and painless that some people I have worked on for anxiety don't really believe that that was all it took and look for other answers as to why their anxiety has left them. It is an amazing tool for helping with emotional stress. I can't recommend it highly enough.

Having your own tools is great but there are times when you just need someone else to take the stress away. I have also found that a session of craniosacral therapy, reiki or acupuncture is fantastic to relax and re-balance the body and so de-stress. I am blessed because my sister Emer recently qualified in Indian head massage and reiki and is so patient with her willing guinea pigs.

One of my favourite de-stressers, however, is very simple and cheap – dancing. As I don't go to clubs so often these days it is mostly confined to my kitchen, with my sisters, Nikki and Emer, and my nieces and nephews. Even Nikki's little two-and-a-half year old, Nathan, runs up to our stereo demanding some music now when he calls out (obviously with his parents – he's not actually driving yet but he's a little genius so any day now). Another one of our wonderful nephews, Shane, will only dance to Christmas songs so if you hear 'Santa Claus Is Coming to Town' coming from my kitchen in June, you know why. I will quite possibly be an acute embarrassment to my nieces and nephews as they get older but in the meantime I will make them dance around my kitchen with me to old music, God love them! I turn on some of my favourite songs and let it all hang out ('My Sharona' by the Knack, 'Sweet Child of Mine' by Guns n' Roses, 'Let's Go Crazy' by Prince

— the list is endless and very eighties so you can imagine my moves). It's great fun, especially if you put on some songs with a great beat that take you back to a time in your life when you were confident that the whole world was your oyster and nothing was impossible. Music can actually bring you back to how you felt then and make it real again. Try it and see. It's a bit of a family tradition anyway. Nikki, Emer and I have great memories from our childhood of dancing around the kitchen with our mum.

Of course, when you start trying to conceive, this can be stressful in itself. For me, I can relax once I know I am doing something positive towards my goal, but I know not everyone is the same. Be happy and focus on today and how great your life is already. If you have any issues in your life, do whatever you have to do to sort them out. Working through any emotional issues before you conceive can help you to become a happier parent. Don't ever think that having a baby will solve your problems or make you happy if you are not already happy in yourself. Babies should not be born to fill a hole in your life. But when they come along you make room for them because I believe your heart gets bigger. Children are extremely hard work, but of course bring you enormous joy.

In my own efforts to cover all the bases, I went to see a hypnotherapist one time. I actually had it in my mad head that my body was so used to failing at pregnancy that it could be hypnotised into being good at it. However, I ended up having three sessions to work out my issues with my dad, who left us when I was four. I had thought that I was over it, as it happened so long ago, but I think that this was a good exercise to help me deal with the emotional issues surrounding that event. I know that that whole issue is now put to rest and not lurking anywhere in the background. It wasn't my immediate fertility solution but I'm still glad I did it.

If you have ever read Dermot O'Connor's excellent book, *The Healing Code*, he recommends dealing with any internal emotional issues you may have from your past as part of a healing process. Counselling and life coaching are really helpful options. The thing to do is to open your mind to dealing with your emotional baggage and the right method for doing this (for you) will become apparent and you will be most attracted to it. Live lighter. Think of it like flying with Ryanair – you can only carry on so much (emotional) baggage or you will end up paying the price. Poor health is the price you pay for too much stress, so dealing with stress is a vitally important aspect of the three-month plan, just like the €56 I ended up paying Ryanair when I was on my way *out* to Spain one time, because I thought I needed a different handbag for every outfit. I have now invested in a luggage scale for travelling and like to think of my EFT and other de-stressing tools as my emotional luggage scale.

Health Check

This seems so sensible to me now that I don't know why I didn't think of it when I first decided to have a baby, but hindsight is always twenty-twenty vision. Go for a health check with your GP. Have your blood pressure checked and a full blood count taken, especially of your thyroid function, iron levels, Vitamin B levels and hormones – oestrogen, FSH, LH, prolactin, progesterone, and so on. All of the above terms are explained in the glossary at the back of this book. Have this blood test done on the seventh day after ovulation. If there is something that isn't right why wait until you have been unsuccessfully trying to conceive for a couple of months to find out? For the sake of a quick blood test, get it sorted now before you even start to try. Ask for, keep and file a copy of all of your results. Do not be put off if your doctor thinks that you are being over-fussy by requesting blood tests at this stage. It is only sensible to have a medical check at the start and if anything is off balance you can address it immediately to give yourself the best possible chance of success.

Smoking

It is 2013 and the ill effects of smoking on both women and their unborn children are well known. Yet still some people do not or cannot give up smoking during pregnancy. It may be none of my business, but I find I become enraged when I see a pregnant woman smoking. Obviously cigarettes are addictive and can be extremely difficult to give up, but hopefully the information below will give you the extra push to stop smoking. If you absolutely cannot quit then at the very least try to cut down the number of cigarettes you smoke as much as possible. The reasons not to smoke bear repeating, as follows:

- It is known that cigarette smoke contains a mixture of approximately 4,000 chemicals, which include cyanide, lead, nicotine, carbon monoxide and at least 60 carcinogenic compounds. These are undeniably extremely harmful to an unborn baby. You would not eat these ingredients, so why would you feed them to your unborn child? Smoking also reduces the oxygen level in your blood, which deprives your baby of oxygen and can cause a host of health problems for both you and them.
- Women who smoke during pregnancy run a higher risk of miscarriage and are more likely to develop complications in pregnancy and labour and increase the risk of birth defects (including heart defects) and still births and, most frightening of all, smoking during pregnancy can

actually treble the risk of sudden infant death syndrome (cot death).

- Smokers are three times more likely to have small babies. Babies with low birth weights run a higher risk of disease in infancy and early childhood. Babies and children whose parents smoke are twice as likely to develop respiratory problems such as asthma and bronchitis. Every year in the UK, 17,000 children under five are admitted to hospital suffering from the effects of passive smoking.
- Smoking during pregnancy can have lifelong effects on your baby's brain. Children of pregnant smokers have a higher potential to develop learning disorders and behavioural problems, and relatively low IQs.

If you are a smoker and have even considered *not* quitting while pregnant, I sincerely hope that the above has opened your eyes. Don't wait until you are pregnant before quitting; it can be difficult enough to kick the habit without the additional hormones and potential stress of pregnancy to exacerbate the problem. You won't regret it. Studies also show that if your partner smokes the passive smoke can increase your risk of miscarriage, so this is a habit your partner needs to kick too.

Even if you smoked at an earlier point during your pregnancy, it is always better to quit now than to continue to smoke. If you did smoke when you were pregnant and now regret it, obviously you really should not do it again, but you cannot change the past, so instead of feeling guilty work out what you can do to improve your child's health now. Supplements like chlorella and spirulina (mentioned above) would be a good idea for a detox and they also have gamma linolenic acid (GLA), which is a healthy fat that helps boost the body's metabolism; you can also find them in forms and dosages that are suitable for children. You could also book your child in for a number of sessions in a salt therapy clinic, if they experience any respiratory problems. This involves spending time in a climate-controlled environment breathing in salt air. The therapy developed after studies showed that breathing in salt air (in seaside areas and in salt caves) can relieve a wide range of respiratory ailments and skin infections. If your child constantly has a runny nose salt therapy can also help to clear this where antibiotics may have failed. To find out more you can visit asthmasociety.ie, the website of the Asthma Society of Ireland. I am not in any way suggesting that any of the above therapies make up for smoking, but they can possibly relieve some of the symptoms that your child may experience. The best thing to do for your baby is to not smoke at all.

The more research I have done, the more aware I have become of how every part of our body interacts with and reacts to things that happen in other parts of our body. It is actually an amazing piece of machinery. The reality is that most of us look after our cars better that we look after our bodies, until we get ill. Maybe the next time we are sending our car in for a service, we should think about doing a little health check on ourselves at the same time. Am I full of energy when I get up in the morning? What are my skin, hair, nails and tongue trying to tell me? We should try to maintain our health and not just fix it when it goes wrong.

Alcohol and Drugs

According to Alcohol Action Ireland (alcoholireland.ie), the most recent advice from the Department of Health's chief medical officer is clear:

Given the harmful drinking patterns in Ireland and the propensity to binge drink, there is a substantial risk of neurological damage to the foetus resulting in Foetal Alcohol Spectrum Disorders (FASD). Therefore, it is in the child's best interest for a pregnant woman not to drink alcohol during pregnancy.

The placenta does not act as a barrier to alcohol and so drinking while pregnant can lead to brain disorders. While the exact amount of alcohol consumption required to cause disorders such as foetal alcohol spectrum disorders (learning, behavioural, social and attention difficulties) is uncertain, there are certainly no health benefits for the baby. The most extreme disorder is foetal alcohol syndrome, where the child is exposed to extreme alcohol consumption. This affects the child's height, central nervous system and facial features. You won't let your child drink for eighteen years (if you are lucky) after they are born, so really you shouldn't drink while they are growing inside you.

Recreational drugs and pregnancy do not mix well. While problems differ depending on the type, quality and quantity of drug you take, illicit drug use during pregnancy can lead to higher risks of miscarriage, birth defects, low birth weight, cot death, an insufficient oxygen supply to your baby, heart defects and placental abruption (a potentially fatal condition where the placenta can separate from the wall of the uterus). Your child may also suffer from withdrawal symptoms after birth and is at a higher risk of developing learning and behavioural problems.

Diabetes and Gestational Diabetes

Glucose is the sugar that is in your blood. It is very important that these levels are not too high or too low. Normal glucose levels are particularly important when you are trying to conceive so that you can avoid the complication of gestational diabetes, which will affect the health of your unborn baby. Glucose levels in the blood are regulated by a hormone called insulin. Type 1 diabetes occurs when the body cannot make enough insulin and so this must be injected daily. This type is not related to obesity.

However, type 2 diabetes is a growing risk for Irish people due to our modern-day diets and lifestyles. It can cause all sorts of health risks and complications, such as blurry vision, excessive thirst, fatigue, hunger, weight loss, heart attack, stroke, nerve damage and kidney damage. A good healthy diet and exercise are essential, along with whatever treatments are recommended by your doctor.

If you have diabetes and wish to get pregnant, it is more challenging but possible if you work with your doctor and dietician/nutritionist closely. You need to control your blood glucose levels much more tightly during pregnancy, so you may need to check your blood sugars more frequently and your medications may need to be changed or discontinued. Women with diabetes also need to take a higher dose of folic acid during pregnancy than women who don't. More information is available from your doctor and from Diabetes Ireland (www.diabetes.ie/living-with-diabetes/pregnancy-and-diabetes).

Gestational diabetes develops during pregnancy because the mother's body is unable to produce enough insulin. Sometimes, the hormones that occur during pregnancy can block the action of insulin. This means that the amount of sugar in the blood rises. These high blood sugar levels pass to the baby through the placenta and can cause health issues. This form of diabetes usually starts during the second half of pregnancy and resolves itself after the birth of the baby. If you have gestational diabetes you need to have regular blood sugar (glucose) tests carried out. Controlling your blood sugar levels is essential and can be done through a combination of diet and exercise, and possibly insulin injections.

You Are Ready to Try

So you have carried out your preparations, are fit and healthy and know your cycle inside out. You are eating the right food for you and maintaining a healthy weight. The time is right to really start trying to get pregnant now. How exciting! Of course, you are going to try to conceive when the timing is right, i.e. particularly from three days before ovulation until the day after. It is worth noting that the best time to try to conceive is actually just before ovulation because sperm can survive for up to five days in the womb (hardy little bucks!). As you only have a limited window of opportunity once the egg has been released, it makes sense that there is a better chance if the 'boys' are *in situ* ready and waiting. However, remember that you shouldn't just have sex for the sake of getting pregnant. Keep your relationship alive and healthy during the rest of the month too and make sure that this important part of your relationship is still very much about the two of you and not solely about conceiving. Remember, it will eventually be just the two of you again someday when the kids have fled the nest, and even when you are in the middle of raising a family it is important to maintain the central relationship between mother and father. Raising a family is time-consuming and stressful, so it is important to be able to laugh with and rely on your partner. If you are happy then your children will be too, so never lose sight of each other in all of this.

Keep positive and try not to get too upset if it doesn't happen straight away, even though it can be really frustrating. Keep charting your cycle so that you have a good record in case you need it and keep up with your supplements and healthy lifestyle. I have found it really annoying when people have told me to relax because I wanted my baby *now*. However, at this stage there is nothing to worry about because you are doing all you should and have had all of the basics checked out. Just enjoy your sleep while you can!

I know that most of you will conceive quite quickly and won't need to read on any further for yourselves and I am so happy for you. However, increasing statistics are unfortunately showing that you will more than likely at least *know* someone who will face challenges when it comes to starting their own family. I have included some of my own experiences in the following sections to explain what the treatments and the emotions involved are like. Hang on to this little book in case it might help you to help them in certain circumstances. Life is all the richer when you take some time to understand and help someone else. I wish you all the very best and hope you will get pregnant in 'jig time', as Dessie says!

2

Six Months On and I'm Not Pregnant Yet

Feeling Stressed and Frustrated

OK, so you have been trying to conceive for six months and are not pregnant yet. There is no need to panic at this stage but I know that you are naturally feeling frustrated and stressed. Every month is a disappointment when your period comes and you feel desperately impatient for your next ovulation so that you can try again. I would say that if you have been charting, know that you are having sex at the right times and have taken all of the preparatory steps recommended in Chapter 1, then after six months you should go to see your GP. I say six months because more and more of us are only starting our families in our thirties and if there is a deeper problem you want to get it diagnosed and treated as quickly as possible. You will probably become pregnant while you are doing this but at least no time will have been wasted. Do not let the fear of a problem stop you from finding it and dealing with it head on. There are terrific solutions to most problems once you know what they are. Being informed gives you the power to solve problems. Where there is a will there is a way, and fear will only waste your time and energy.

Back to Your GP

Ensure that you have a good rapport with your GP and that they listen to you and take your concerns seriously. Remember that doctors are normal people, just like you and me, and so they are all different. Some will have a positive interest in the area of fertility. If yours does not, then find another doctor who does. Don't forget that you know your own body better than any doctor and if you are listening to it you can provide them with valuable information. Your chart will also be a great help and may provide valuable information. If your GP tries to persuade you to wait until you have been trying for a year and tells you that it is too early to check things out yet, insist that you want to be checked out further *now*. Remember that this is your life and your time that could be wasted if there is a problem to be solved.

Blood Tests and Scans

Your doctor will probably repeat the same blood tests done for your health check (see Chapter 1) seven days post ovulation and should take another blood sample on Day 3 of your cycle. They should also arrange for you to have an ultrasound scan to check for fibroids and ovarian cysts. This is also the time to have your partner's sperm count checked just to be sure. Again, I would urge you to get a copy of and keep a file of all these results and learn about them for yourself.

I have listed and explained briefly in layman's terms some of the more common issues which may be discovered in Chapter 3. This information is obviously not a definitive medical guide as I am not medically trained, but I hope that it will give you enough information so that you can ask more informed questions of your medical team to help you fully understand what you need to do. Also, I want to make sure that you leave no stone unturned in your efforts to get a diagnosis and you can only do that when you know what the stones are.

Selecting Your Fertility Specialist

Once your GP has carried out the basic tests, depending on what is or is not discovered, they may refer you to a specialist. However, bear in mind that some GPs are familiar with certain fertility specialists and clinics and refer their patients to the same ones all the time. Ask them who they propose to refer you to and, before they do, go away and do some research on them yourself. While all clinics and specialists are of course good, you need to find the one who can diagnose and solve *your* individual problem. You could potentially spend a lot of money on the wrong team for you. If you are considering attending a fertility clinic, I would recommend that you choose one which takes a holistic approach to your treatment, i.e. makes sure that your general health is good, that you are in the right frame of mind, that you are emotionally ready for your treatment and that they have diagnosed what the issues are with regards to your fertility. There are several reputable clinics around the country and you should get a full list and interview the ones you are attracted to.

I would really recommend reading *Is Your Body Baby-Friendly?* by Alan E. Beer. I have only recently come across this book and it was a revelation to me due to my immune problems. I realised some time ago that my food intolerances and endometriosis created a serious problem with my immune system, but when I suggested this to my doctor at the time I received what I can only describe as a 'watery' response. Reading Dr Beer's book was fantastic because it vindicated what my own intuition had been telling me and helped restore my confidence in myself. Dr Beer states in the book that he faced opposition for his ideas, but he had amazing success in the United States with couples for whom IVF had previously failed. I would suggest reading the book and learning all you can from it, and then discussing it with your chosen specialist. Your immune system may not be your problem but you will still definitely be more informed about the whole process and so ask better questions.

Make an informed decision as to which specialist you and your partner both like. Obviously things like cost and location will also be a factor. Check out reviews and see if you can get some referrals. Find out as much as you can before you commit. Ask the specialists about their experience, diagnosis process, success rates with your particular issues and age group, and hidden charges. Do not be intimidated or make a decision when you are in a desperate frame of mind. Be logical. You will be spending a lot of money so you need to spend it wisely and on a method with the best chance of success. Treatments are very hard on you and the success statistics are less than 35 per cent (in some cases a lot less, depending on age), so be smart.

One bugbear that I have with regard to fertility clinics is that some have the walls of their reception areas covered in baby photographs. The first time I saw one of these, it made me feel warm and fuzzy and excited. I dreamed of adding our photo to that wall. However, when you consider the success rates, this wall of photographs to me now is a promise that the clinic cannot guarantee it can keep. We attended a fertility clinic where I was treated for endometriosis and then became pregnant. When I lost our baby, I couldn't walk back in there to face that wall, which only served to remind me of my own failure. I really think that such photos would be better placed in the staff canteen instead. These photographs are painful to look at for over two-thirds of their patients. This is not to diminish the amazing work that fertility clinics do and how happy they make their successful clients. I just think that there has to be a way to improve their success rates and the holistic approach, combined with us taking an informed part in our own treatment, as early as possible, has to help.

NaPro Technology

Natural Procreative Technology (NaPro) is a programme for couples experiencing difficulty with fertility. It is a reproductive science that focuses on recording and understanding the natural fertility cycle so that abnormalities can be identified and treated through changes in lifestyle, and hormonal, medical and surgical intervention, enabling you to conceive naturally. We took part in this programme in the past. What I really like about it is that it investigates and deals with underlying health issues as well as carrying out the usual tests for polycystic ovary syndrome (PCOS), fibroids and endometriosis (see Chapter 3 for more details).

NaPro is not generally a quick fix. It can be an eighteen-month programme, although many couples become pregnant before that time. This is difficult when you want your baby *now*. I had a few issues to work through and so we were in the programme for over a year. You need patience and faith and the knowledge that because the building blocks for your fertility are being corrected, you are being given the best chance for success.

I had become aware of my gluten intolerance through the Turner Clinic in Dublin but further blood tests with the NaPro programme revealed my many other intolerances mentioned in Chapter 1. I learned how to manage these intolerances and eventually have been able to re-introduce some of these foods on occasion. I also had monthly blood tests to monitor my hormone levels and was on hormone support drugs (some of which I injected). I had a laparoscopy (a keyhole procedure where a small camera is used to inspect the uterus, ovaries and fallopian tubes) some months ago and although I have been left with one clubbed tube because of the endometriosis, the plumbing is otherwise in good shape now and there is still hope. In between visits to my doctor, I saw my NaPro practitioner every few months, who taught me how to chart and much more besides about my fertility cycle and supplements and so on. I have learned so much about my own individual fertility since first attending Dr Olga at the Turner Clinic, charting with Maybe Baby and then joining the NaPro programme. Once I started on this learning curve, I felt compelled to carry out my own research and learn even more. It makes such perfect sense to me now to know and under-stand my own individual physiology. I just wish I had realised this in the early days. We are now quite hopeful as we have ticked many boxes and things look good. However, I am not kidding myself and know that every year of my age is against me and, as I am on the wrong side of 40, I wish I had known when I started what I know now. However, all we need is one good egg (two would be nice).

One thing that I would suggest to anyone considering the NaPro programme, if there is a good chance that you might have endometriosis and so need surgery, seriously discuss with your doctor if there is any point in starting to take fertility drugs before the laparoscopy. I have found fertility drugs to be very hard on me emotionally and physically and the less time you have to be on them the better. After my last laparoscopy, my drugs were increased, probably with the intention of making something happen quickly – an approach which I am sure has worked for many women – but I reacted badly (it appears I have a very sensitive system) and I feel that I lost some valuable time dealing with side effects that left it unlikely that I would conceive while on the drugs. However, I still believe in the NaPro approach. The success rates are good and I think that even if it does not work for you and you feel that you need IVF at the end of it, which you would have to do in another clinic, you would be in good shape for the best chance of success. There is no perfect solution out there for everybody so you have to find the best mix of treatments for *you*. You can get more information about NaPro on www.fertilitycare.ie.

Diagnosis, Diagnosis, Diagnosis

I cannot emphasise strongly enough how important diagnosis is. Diagnosis is your friend because it informs you what you need to do next. It is my humble belief there is no point in going straight for IVF without having diagnosed the underlying problem, even when it is so tempting to do so because you are so impatient for your baby and it seems like the quickest route to success. I fully understand the obsessive impatience. We were booked in for IVF treatment at one point but I became pregnant and so cancelled it. However, I always knew that my problem was not getting pregnant but staying pregnant and so, while IVF is a brilliant miracle of modern science, it is not the answer for everyone, and I believe that couples spend thousands of Euro on treatments that have no hope of success because their undiagnosed underlying problem or health issue has not been treated. When you know what you are dealing with you can select the medical expert and alternative therapist to suit you. As soon as a doctor seems at a loss to know what the problem is, research who is at the forefront of fertility issues and go to see them or at least contact them for information and advice.

A doctor once said to me 'and if this doesn't work you might decide to stop.' I didn't say anything at the time because I wasn't sure what I wanted to do and I thought I really needed the prescription that he was writing for me (I sound like a drug addict!) but that was the last time I saw him. He obviously was not very invested in whether we succeeded or not. It really is not up to your doctor to tell you when you should stop trying completely. Of course, they can say that they are not sure what to do next and so maybe you need a different specialist, but at least such doctors recognise the limitations of their own knowledge and are trying to help you find the appropriate specialist.

On another occasion, I was told by a specialist that there was no point in my having another laparoscopy as they thought that my problem was purely my age. In fairness, I didn't have obvious symptoms but I had had endometriosis before and in most cases it comes back. I had a very early appointment and remember sitting outside the clinic in my car afterwards crying my eyes out on the phone to Dessie. I then turned on the breakfast show on the radio only to hear Hector's birth notices on 2FM – the name of the baby, the size of the baby and the parish of the baby. This felt like salt being rubbed in my wounds. So I decided to have the surgery and the specialist sheepishly admitted afterwards that the surgery had been worth it as they had found extensive endometriosis.

Trust yourself and keep looking for your diagnosis. If the worst-case scenario happens and there is absolutely no hope, at least you have the option of considering adoption at this stage, which you cannot do unless you have stopped trying for your own baby.

When I find the going tough, I always think of this quote from Dr Alan Beer and it gives me great hope and comfort:

'You have nothing to fear. If there is a problem, we will know. If there is not a problem, we will rejoice. The most important thing is to know that what is wrong with you is not your fault. It has a specific cause and understanding that cause fully brings with it the power to persist and move onward, even though the fear of failure will never leave you.'

Alan E. Beer, *Is Your Body Baby-Friendly?*, Introduction, p. xxxiii.

We had thought of going to his clinic in Chicago to see Dr Beer for treatment because of his success with immune-related fertility issues, but he sadly passed away in 2006, just weeks before his book was published. However, he has left behind his knowledge and a legacy of over 7,000 couples whom he has successfully helped to have their own families. In a chapter called 'Helping to Explain the Unexplained', Dr Beer says, 'I do not see myself as one who knows all the answers. However, I do hold my experience as almost sacred to me, for I have acquired it from patients like many of you who are reading this' – how humble and lovely. We absolutely must be part of our own solution and must be a part of our own medical team. That means learning as much as we can, offering suggestions that come from our own instincts, challenging our doctors when we need to and giving feedback to doctors and therapists.

Having corresponded with a couple of specialists and resolved my health issues, we have decided that if we do not get pregnant soon, we will go ahead with IVF in a clinic which recognises the role of the immune system in fertility. Because of my clubbed tube, it might speed things up for us. However, I would not even make an appointment to see any specialist now without getting some further information from them and finding out who they are and as much information about what they do as possible. We have narrowed our choice down to two who were respectful enough to answer my questions and correspond with me on the subject. I would probably have felt that it was too cheeky in the past to question a specialist about their work but just remember – our time, our money.

Do not ever forget that miracles happen too. I have heard stories where people were given no hope and ended up having perfectly healthy babies. Life is good and we are great when we are balanced, healthy and open-minded.

Tests

The following section explains some of the more common tests that you might come across while your infertility is being investigated.

Laparoscopy and Dye

If your other tests (i.e. blood tests and scans for fibroids and ovarian cysts) have come back clear, once you have been referred to a fertility clinic or specialist you may be advised to have a laparoscopy and dye test. This entails investigative keyhole surgery which looks for abnormalities inside the womb and checks that your fallopian tubes are clear by pumping dye through them, which will show up any obstructions. Obviously you are under a general anaesthetic for this procedure. Because gas is pumped into your abdomen so that the surgeon can see your organs clearly, there can some discomfort afterwards. I have had two 'lap and dyes' and it took a little longer to get over the second one, purely because the surgeon had more work to do the second time round. After the first one, I was up out of bed after two days, although I took a week off work; after the second one, I didn't get out of bed for six days. Remember that after undergoing surgery it is important to ensure that you eat well (lots of fruit and vegetables) and drink plenty of water.

Antral Follicle Count

This is a test which can be carried out to determine how many eggs you have left in your reserve. The antral follicles are small follicles (2–8mm in diameter) at the latter stage of maturation that can be measured using an ultrasound. This test can also predict the expected response to ovarian stimulation and therefore the chance of successful pregnancy with IVF. More information is available at www.advancedfertility.com/antralfollicles.htm.

Anti-Mullerian Hormone Testing

Anti-mullerian hormone (AMH) is a hormone produced by granulosa cells in the ovarian follicles. The levels of AMH in the blood are thought to reflect the size of the remaining egg supply. This blood test can be carried out on any day of your cycle. More information is available at www.advancedfertility.com/amh-fertility-test.htm.

(Just a personal note on the above two tests. I was offered these tests and didn't take them as I was afraid that if the results were considered to be low, it would only add to my stress and reduce my optimism. After all, you only need one egg! While I fully understand that higher results increase your chances and some people need to know facts and figures regarding their chances, personally I don't and so my advice is to really think about all of the tests that you are offered and if they will help or hinder you personally. We are all different and all know our own individual strengths so work to these.)

Chromosomal Testing

Chromosome analysis looks at your chromosomes, which are the packages of DNA inside your cells, under a microscope. If you think of your DNA as a library, each chromosome is a book and your genes are the chapters inside each book. Each chapter, or gene, contains a specific instruction for your body. One chromosome may contain hundreds or thousands of genes. You can't see individual genes under a microscope, but you can see the chromosomes that hold them.

Most humans have 46 chromosomes. Chromosomes are inherited in pairs: one set of 23 chromosomes comes from the mother through the egg, and the other set comes from the father through the sperm. There are 22 pairs of numbered chromosomes (called autosomes) plus one pair of sex chromosomes (the X and Y chromosomes).

Chromosome analysis can tell if all or part of a chromosome is missing, extra or rearranged. Too much or too little genetic information from the numbered chromosomes usually causes birth defects and/or mental retardation. Abnormalities of the sex chromosomes may cause reproductive problems, but some people with sex chromosome abnormalities go through life without knowing they have any problems. Chromosome analysis does not find problems with how individual genes work (for example, genetic diseases like cystic fibrosis, Tay–Sachs disease and sickle cell anaemia).

This is a subject around which there is some debate. I am naturally always watching out for developments in fertility treatments. As I am no spring chicken, I feel the need to be informed about every option that is out there so that we can make a judgement as to whether it is something that we would like to explore. There has been some controversy recently about chromosomal testing because some people are of the opinion that it is somehow discriminating against disabled people and could be used by couples to pick perfect babies, determine gender and so on. However, as I see it, the majority of fertility doctors use this technology to help couples like us, who have been unable to carry a pregnancy to term, select the egg that has the best chance of survival. I think that it would be discrimination against us, or any other couple in our position, who have been through miscarriages and fertility hell, if we were perceived as being immoral for using this science to improve the chance of having our own baby. Many treatments can be used for good or can be abused, even to the point of causing death, such as many prescription drugs, but the benefits offered by these drugs outweigh the problems caused by misuse or abuse. Just as patients and doctors must be trusted to choose the treatment that is right for them, couples in our situation should be afforded the respect to make informed choices and to decide for ourselves what is moral or not.

Treatments

This section explains some of the more common treatments for infertility.

Intrauterine Insemination

Intrauterine insemination (IUI) is an infertility treatment which places the best quality sperm in the uterus to improve the chances of the sperm reaching and fertilising an egg in the fallopian tube. It is not terribly invasive and often doesn't require too much medication. The woman has internal ultrasounds to track her follicle development and identify the best day to carry out the procedure. The man's semen is analysed in a laboratory to identify the sperm most likely to succeed and this is placed in the uterus by a gynaecologist on the day that the egg is ready to be fertilised. There is a follow-up ultrasound to confirm the pregnancy a few weeks later.

In Vitro Fertilisation

In vitro fertilisation (IVF) is a treatment where drugs are used to induce an artificial menopause, followed by high doses of hormones to stimulate the ovaries. The woman's eggs are then harvested or retrieved and the man's sperm is collected, usually on the same day. Specialists will analyse both in a lab and put the best sperm and eggs together for fertilisation. Three to five days later a number of fertilised eggs will be transferred back into the uterus. This procedure also involves taking a large number of fertility drugs and self-injections. On that note, I never thought I could inject myself. However, you will do anything that you have to and it is honestly not hard at all once you have done it the first time. It is not even sore. It is actually harder to deal with the raging hormones and emotions that accompany IVF.

Intracytoplasmic sperm injection (ICSI) is a form of IVF where a single sperm is injected directly into the egg. This method is used when the sperm count is very low or the quality or motility of the sperm is poor.

Acupuncture can prove to be helpful to couples going through IVF. The above is merely an outline of what is involved but the clinics will go through their procedures step by step, and you should really study them as, if you decide to use IVF, these procedures will have a big impact on your life.

You should interview several clinics before you decide which one is the best fit for you.

Complementary Therapies

Once you know what the problem is, if any, you can then also investigate complementary therapies such as acupuncture, craniosacral therapy, reflexology and Maya womb massage, which can really help. Again the information which you have kept from all of your tests will help your therapist to decide if and how they can help you. If you are on fertility medication, just be wary of taking Chinese herbs at the same time – check with your doctor first. Also, keep your doctor informed about any therapies you are having so that the results of these can be measured or taken into account in your treatment. Complementary therapies can help by calming your emotions and improving your energy and vitality.

Acupuncture

Acupuncture is a method of encouraging the body to promote natural healing and improve functioning by inserting needles and applying heat or electrical stimulation at very precise acupuncture points. It is an ancient Chinese healing method which is based on the belief that channels of energy run in regular patterns through the body and over its surface. These energy channels, called meridians, are like rivers flowing through the body to irrigate and nourish the tissues. An obstruction in the movement of these energy rivers can cause illness or disease.

The acupuncture needles, inserted at the relevant points, unblock the obstructions and re-establish the regular flow of energy through the meridians. Acupuncture treatments can, it is argued, help the body's internal organs to correct imbalances in digestion, absorption and energy production activities, including fertility, and in the circulation of energy through the meridians. The improved energy and biochemical balance produced by acupuncture stimulates the body's natural healing abilities and promotes physical and emotional well-being.

Craniosacral Therapy

Craniosacral therapy was developed in the 1970s by John Upledger, an American osteopathic physician, building on the work of William Sutherland, who founded the field of cranial osteopathy in the 1930s. Sutherland noticed the importance of cranial (head) bone mobility as well as the effects that restrictions in this area had throughout the whole body.

'The craniosacral system' is the term used to describe the physiological body system which consists of the membranes and cerebrospinal fluid that surround and protect the brain and spinal cord, extending from the bones of the skull (which make up the cranium) down to the tailbone area (or sacrum). The theory of craniosacral therapy states that the role of this system in the development and performance of the brain and spinal cord is so vital that an imbalance or dysfunction in it can cause sensory, motor and/or neurological disabilities. The therapy consists of gentle palpation or massage of the body at key points to monitor the rhythm of the craniosacral system and unblock any restrictions in the flow of cerebrospinal fluid, thus enhancing the body's natural capacity for healing. The therapist may also just lightly touch or cradle certain areas, like the head or the base of the spine, and allow their healing energies to flow through.

Some therapists use craniosacral therapy to encourage a healthy conception and pregnancy by regulating hormonal imbalances via the pituitary gland, reducing physical tensions and relieving stress levels. Craniosacral therapy is believed to help enhance vitality and healthy functioning of the reproductive organs by releasing restrictions, such as scar tissue, in the surrounding connective tissues for both men and women within the pelvic region. It is also helpful for gynaecological problems. Craniosacral therapy can be used in conjunction with IVF or other medical treatments. It can also help reduce pain, discomfort and bloating from the drugs associated with IVF.

While researching craniosacral therapy, I found a clinic in Florida called Clear Passage which uses massage to treat scar tissue and has had great success in dealing with many conditions, including fertility-related ones. This has made me more convinced that, while craniosacral therapy is more gentle than massage, it can help to heal scar tissue and so can help me and others who suffer from scar tissue.

Reflexology

Often mistaken for a foot massage, reflexology is an ancient healing therapy that accesses some of the 7,000 nerve endings in the foot, which are linked to every organ and system of the body. Through skilful manipulation, a reflexologist can help to unblock the flow of energy in organs and rebalance your system. It is particularly useful for stress-related conditions as it helps to counteract the negative effects of stress and stimulate the body's own healing process. It is argued that reflexology not only aids recovery but can help the body to maintain health. As some points on the foot are associated with a woman's egg production, by manipulating these areas reflexologists claim they can correct the imbalances which can cause infertility.

Maya Womb Massage

The Arvigo Techniques of Maya Abdominal Therapy (AT-MAT) includes a number of therapies, one of which is Maya womb massage. Maya womb massage is a non-invasive uterus massage carried out over the abdomen which brings the uterus back to its proper position. This ancient practice is still used today in Mexico and Central America by traditional healers and midwives. It is said to heal and prevent menstrual disorders, chronic miscarriage and infertility. It is also used during pregnancy, labour and postpartum care to ensure that the womb is returned to its proper position to avoid the pain of displacement. It is claimed that AT-MAT benefits the digestive system and the male reproductive system. AT-MAT is recommended by some fertility specialists and acupuncturists to help increase women's chances of conceiving and having successful pregnancies.

I was recently told by an energy healer that my womb was very displaced. She worked on it for me and apparently all is as it should be now. Having tried Maya womb massage, I must say my posture has definitely improved and afterwards my periods were painless, whereas before I would have experienced some cramping for two days. This displacement may have happened as far back as childhood from a fall or accident. I have also had surgeries on this area like laparoscopies and D&Cs (dilation and curettage – a gynaecological procedure sometimes used after a miscarriage to remove the foetus from the uterus), which are traumatic to your body, and I think in hindsight that some therapy (reiki/craniosacral therapy) or this Maya womb massage would have been a really helpful thing to do afterwards to help my energy system and organs return to normal. I have also been intrigued to discover that a displaced uterus may be a factor in progressing endometriosis, among other fertility issues.

Apparently, having Maya womb massage during pregnancy can help position the baby for a gentler delivery, and it may decrease nausea, urinary tract infections, hip and lower back pain, acid reflux and the chance of haemorrhage. It may also improve circulation, digestion and craniosacral rhythm. Having postnatal Maya womb massage can heal, lift, strengthen and balance the uterus, ligaments and pelvic floor muscles, prevent a tilted or prolapsed uterus, soften C-section scar tissue and correct incontinence. For more information see www.fertilehands.com or www.mayatherapy.ie.

The Internet

In conjunction with other sources, I have used the internet for the purposes of getting more information. I recommend sticking with the medical websites. You can also find interesting studies published by doctors online. However, always remember that it is a bad idea to self-diagnose by reading too many symptoms lists and so on. Use the information you find as the basis for discussions with your medical team so that you can ask more informed questions, and never decide that you have a certain condition before you have been diagnosed with it. Let's face it, some symptoms can belong to a long list of illnesses or health issues. However, all hail wonderful Google!

Conclusion

Take responsibility for your own situation and be your own project manager. Don't assume that your GP or gynaecologist knows everything about fertility or about what solutions are out there (unless of course you have gone straight to the top specialist). I was under a consultant and then a gynaecologist who told me I was fine after having been treated for endometriosis the first time and neither of whom told me that there is a very high incidence of it recurring as quickly as within six months of treatment. They also did not mention the link between diet and endometriosis and how the correct diet can help enormously. Time was lost because they did not fully inform me and I did not ask enough questions. Question and interrogate as much as you need to until you fully understand your issues, and then research some more. Once you know what you need to do, focus on achieving perfect health.

Unfortunately, everyone's story is different so the above is really the only and best advice I can give you when it comes to finding your solution to your particular problem. Hopefully, it will help you to get to the root of things quickly, but no matter how fast it is it will feel like longer than you can bear on occasion.

Chapters 4 and 5 of this book are all about the emotional side of this subject, which is a huge part of fertility issues. I also include some basic details on some of the more common problems facing women when trying to conceive in Chapter 3, which you should only read if you are facing a problem – you don't want to start out thinking negatively about everything that could go wrong! This book is not a comprehensive medical guide by any stretch of the imagination, but I hope that it will help to open your mind to asking questions and assisting your medical team to find the solution to your problem. Stay strong and positive as much as you can and be kind to yourself on the difficult days. Keep good people around you and remember always that life is good. Find something to laugh about as often as you can and laugh as heartily as you can because life goes by in a flash. Do everything in your power to make sure your dream comes true but enjoy and live your life today. Do not be defined or destroyed by the challenges that face you in life.

This is a great quote from a lady with whom we are all familiar that always gives me encouragement:

'When I thought I couldn't go on, I forced myself to keep going. My success is based on persistence, not luck.'

Estee Lauder

This is another great quote which I found in Dr Beer's book and was one of the reasons why I like it so much:

'The purpose of science is to change belief! If you believe that infertility, IVF failure, recurrent miscarriages, prematurity, and low birthweight are "God's will", which is not testable scientifically, you will never try to find effective treatment.'

Sir Peter Medawar (Nobel laureate)

Good luck and keep persisting!

3

Fertility Challenges

This chapter offers some basic information about physical conditions which affect fertility. When you leave no stone unturned to discover your issue, you can study it and find out how to fix it and who is the best doctor or therapist to help you do this. Obviously I'm not a medical expert so the information in this chapter has been gathered from my research over the years. A list of websites giving more information about all the issues discussed below is included in the back of this book.

Miscarriage

'Miscarriage' is the term used when a pregnancy ends on its own within the first twenty weeks. There can often be many confusing emotions that accompany the grief of a miscarriage, and the reasons can be varied and are not always identified. In most cases women will become pregnant again within a year and have a perfectly healthy baby.

Missed Miscarriage

I hate this particular title. It sounds like it has slipped your mind that you were supposed to miscarry, which does not describe the enormity of what happens when your baby dies inside you. A missed miscarriage is where the embryo fails to develop but, unlike a 'normal' miscarriage, it is not expelled from your body. This is usually discovered during an ultrasound scan when a heartbeat cannot be found. A D&C is then scheduled to remove your little baby from you.

Ectopic Pregnancy

An ectopic pregnancy occurs when a fertilised egg implants somewhere other than in the wall of the uterus, most frequently in the fallopian tube. Symptoms include bleeding and pelvic or belly pain. As soon as an ectopic pregnancy has been diagnosed with an ultrasound scan it is treated immediately to avoid the possibility of rupture and severe blood loss; this means sadly either medically or surgically ending the pregnancy.

Cornual (Interstitial) Pregnancy

A cornual or interstitial pregnancy is a rare type of ectopic pregnancy. This is where the fertilised egg is implanted deep in the wall where the fallopian tubes reach the uterus. It can be difficult to diagnose on a normal scan but new technology such as 4D scans can locate exactly where the embryo is located. As this type of pregnancy is considered to be a medical emergency, surgical removal is required. Laparoscopic procedures are now being used more often and are less risky than traditional surgery through the abdomen.

Molar Pregnancy

A molar pregnancy is a conception where something goes wrong at the very beginning (misconception). It is a type of trophoblastic disease and is very uncommon. The name is derived from the trophoblasts, which are cells that make up the placenta. The foetus and placenta usually develop together but with a molar pregnancy the trophoblasts develop into an abnormal growth in the uterus. Sometimes there is no developing foetus present; other times there is but the foetus is genetically abnormal and cannot survive outside the womb. The molar pregnancy is also known as a hydatidiform mole. Once detected, a molar pregnancy should be removed immediately, as there is a chance it can grow and spread through your blood into other parts of the body. Molar pregnancies are usually benign but in rare cases can become cancerous. A molar pregnancy is treated by removing the growth through suction or a D&C. You will then receive follow-up blood tests for a number of months to confirm your hormone levels have returned to normal and the entire hydatidiform mole has been removed. You should discuss with your doctor when it is safe to start trying again. The risk of a molar pregnancy recurring is only 1 per cent and the vast majority of couples go on to have healthy babies.

Fibroids

Uterine fibroids are non-cancerous growths that often develop in your uterus during childbearing years. They are also called fibromyomas, leiomyomas or myomas. They are not associated with an increased risk of uterine cancer. They are quite common, often cause no symptoms and can be diagnosed during a pelvic exam or ultrasound. If they require treatment, surgical procedures can shrink or remove them in cases where they cause discomfort or troublesome symptoms, such as pelvic pain or prolonged periods. Although they are not dangerous, they can lead to complications such as anaemia from resulting heavy periods. They do not always interfere with pregnancy. However, if they are blocking the fallopian tubes, or interfere with the passage of sperm from the cervix to the fallopian tubes, they may cause a problem. Sub-mucosal fibroids (those which grow into the inner cavity of the uterus) may prevent implantation of a fertilised egg, and in these cases doctors may remove them before you attempt to get pregnant.

Polycystic Ovary Syndrome

Polycystic ovary syndrome (PCOS) is a common condition where women have an imbalance of female sex hormones (oestrogen and progesterone). This can cause missed or irregular periods and small cysts (fluid-filled sacs) to develop in or on the ovaries. PCOS is most likely genetic so be particularly aware if anyone in your family has suffered or is suffering from symptoms of PCOS. I have read that many women with PCOS have too much insulin in their bodies. This excess of insulin appears to increase the production of androgen, which is a male sex hormone. This is turn can be a cause of acne, excessive hair growth, weight gain and ovulation problems. In women with PCOS, the cyst-covered ovaries cannot produce enough hormones for the egg to fully mature. Because of the high levels of insulin in the body, women with PCOS are also more likely to have diabetes.

I know several women who suffer from PCOS and have been treated successfully for it and now have their babies. I also know of a case where a GP told a woman that she would never have children because of her PCOS, which is simply not for him to say without further investigation by a specialist in this area. There are a number of options to treat the different symptoms of PCOS. Weight gain and obesity can be common in women with PCOS, but losing just 5 per cent of your body weight can improve your hormone, insulin, blood pressure and cholesterol levels, making it easier to become pregnant.

Hormonal medications that stimulate your ovaries can be prescribed to help you get pregnant. Doctors can also provide treatments to regulate your periods, prevent the development of diabetes and reduce excessive hair growth. IVF can also be used by women with PCOS. The message I want to get across is to get a second opinion and do not give up. Reducing your blood glucose levels would also seem to be useful since the condition can be related to high levels of insulin. You can do this by cutting down on sugary processed foods and including foods like lentils and chickpeas, which can help to balance your blood sugars, in your diet. However, every case is different and you should be familiar with the symptoms and causes of PCOS so you can discuss it with the doctor you have chosen to help you.

Endometriosis

Endometriosis is a common gynaecological condition which occurs in up to 15 per cent of all women. It is estimated that 30–45 per cent of women diagnosed with fertility issues will have problems conceiving because of its symptoms. This is also one of my issues and so I have some personal experience of it.

If you have endometriosis, the endometrium, or lining of the womb, grows outside of the womb. It can migrate to the fallopian tubes and ovaries, and can even attach itself to other organs. (This freaked me out at first thinking about this thing sneaking out and being where it shouldn't – a bit like a teenager really!) Although it is outside of the womb, it continues to respond to your hormones and so thickens during the first half of your menstrual cycle and then breaks down at the time of menstruation. However, while the endometrium inside the womb can break down and exit the body through the normal way, i.e. a period, the endometrium which has been displaced breaks down but has nowhere to go and so forms scar tissue on or around whatever organ it is attached to. This is turn causes inflammation, which damages the surrounding tissue over time.

The first time I had a laparoscopy, in 2007, I asked the consultant when he came to see me what he had found. He hurriedly told me that they had found some disease and also that one of my fallopian tubes seemed to have a spasm when they tried to insert some dye. I had to ask him to go back and tell me what disease it was (thinking cancer of course) but he brushed it off and said that they had found some endometriosis but that they had lasered it away and it was gone now so basically forget about it, which I did! When I started in the NaPro programme, my practitioner read my chart and told me that if I had endometriosis before then it was probably back and would possibly have come back within six months. I cannot tell you how devastated I was, as this was September 2010 and so three years had gone by. I had not been told before that there was a high incidence of endometriosis recurring. I had Googled it after the first surgery of course, but just found the definition and did not come across any information about people actually living with it. Of course, we trust that our doctors will tell us everything we need to know.

My new doctor did not recommend a laparoscopy straight away as I have symptomless endometriosis. In fact, the surgeon I attended did not even think I should have surgery because of my 'advanced maternal age'. I was 42 and no woman likes to hear the words 'advanced age'! The decision was left to me and so I decided to have the laparoscopy. The surgeon came to see me afterwards and admitted that it had been worth doing as endometriosis was present and had caused damage to my left fallopian tube. I was put on an experimental drug which doctors in the United States have had some success with in the treatment of autoimmune disorders such as endometriosis, arthritis and multiple sclerosis. I stayed on this medication for about six months, although some women continue taking this medication until menopause in order to manage their symptoms.

The symptoms of endometriosis can vary and include extremely painful periods, backache, nausea, fatigue and gastrointestinal problems. They can occur at any time of the month. Some women, like me, experience no symptoms at all, apart from the inability to maintain a pregnancy, which is, of course, to me the worst one.

Medically, endometriosis is treated with a laser during a laparoscopy. However, you must take a holistic approach and get advice from a dietician or nutritionist who understands this particular issue if you want to have the best chance of relieving your symptoms and preventing the endometriosis from returning. I consulted with Positive Nutrition in Rathmines (positivenutrition.ie), who are excellent and are very interested in fertility issues. As a guideline, they told me to stay away from red meat, dairy products and caffeine and advised me on the correct supplements that I should be taking. They can give you a recommended diet sheet individually tailored for you. There is also an excellent website – www.endometriosis.co.uk – which was set up by Dr Dian Shepperson Mills, an expert in endometriosis, which gives you a lot of information and also a booklet on nutrition which you can download. I can recommend it highly.

Displaced Womb

I was just talking to my mum the other day about all the times we fell about laughing when she shouted at us 'Mind your womb' if we were lifting something too heavy. However, I allowed her to have the last laugh (which of course she didn't do) as I have recently discovered that mine was out of place and may have contributed to my endometriosis (depending on which studies you read).

Our wombs can be displaced as a result of a fall or accident as long ago as during childhood. There are several ways in which it can be displaced:

- Prolapsed (low-lying) – this is most common after going through several pregnancies.
- Side-lying – this can affect ovarian function and so lead to painful and irregular ovulation, ovarian cysts, blocked tubes, circulation problems, hormonal imbalances and difficulty conceiving.
- Retroverted – a tipped-back uterus can block movement in the colon. Constipation, particularly before your period, may result. It can also put pressure on the sacral nerves causing lower back pain.
- Retroflexed – this is a combination of a retroverted uterus and a uterine flexion (where the uterus bends in on itself) (this can happen in any direction and cause painful cramping, and is one possible contributor to endometriosis).
- Anteflexed – a combination of a uterine flexion and anteverted (displaced forward) uterus, which can result in frequent urination, chronic bladder infections and other urinary tract disorders.
- Retrocessed – combination of a prolapsed and a retroverted uterus. The bottom portion of the uterus is lying on the rectum, causing constipation and uncomfortable and painful intercourse.

See also the discussion on Maya womb massage in Chapter 2 and www.fertilehands.com to find out how to treat a displaced womb.

Tubal Problems

The fallopian tubes connect the ovaries to the uterus. Fertilisation typically happens in the fallopian tube, with the fertilised egg then travelling into the uterus to be implanted into the uterine wall. If a tube has been damaged by scar tissue or has become blocked, it can impede the journey of the sperm into the fallopian tube to meet the egg or of the fertilised egg into the uterus for implantation. The scar tissue can be caused by conditions such as endometriosis where the endometrium (lining of the womb) has attached itself to the fallopian tubes. The fallopian tubes can also become blocked by a build-up of fluid (this type of blockage is known as a hydrosalpinx). Treatment depends upon the individual case, where the blockage is and how much damage has been caused. Treatment can include surgical removal of part of the damaged tube or unblocking the tube. After successful treatment, many women go on to have healthy natural pregnancies. In more serious cases, IVF is a viable alternative.

Asherman Syndrome

Asherman syndrome is a condition caused by scars within the uterine cavity (the space within the uterus between the cervical canal and fallopian tubes), which can occur when a D&C is performed. The scars affect the endometrium's ability to grow during the menstrual cycle, leading to fertility challenges. In more serious cases the front and back wall of the uterus stick together. Symptoms of Asherman syndrome can include irregular periods or none at all, although menstrual cramping may be present as if the period had arrived. Other symptoms include recurrent miscarriage and infertility. The scar tissue can be removed using scissors rather than a laser and afterwards your doctor may prescribe oestrogen to encourage healing or insert a balloon into the uterus for a short while to prevent the walls of the uterus from adhering to one another.

Although I did develop some mild scar tissue after my D&C, I do not have this condition; it is not an inevitable result of a D&C, so do not worry unduly if you have had this procedure. I would recommend craniosacral therapy to help heal scar tissue and believe that taking extra Vitamin C and zinc after surgery would be beneficial to help your body to heal. There are several grades of Asherman syndrome and depending on the severity of the case pregnancy can be possible. Your doctor can advise you on the best way for each individual case to proceed once the severity of the disease has been established.

Over-Active Immune System

The immune system plays an important part in fighting the formation of free radicals and foreign invasion by bacteria and viruses. Any infection or allergic reaction in the body can cause over-production of antibodies leading to the immune system attacking the foetus or the sperm, which obviously can cause serious problems when trying to conceive. This is why it is so important to check for food intolerances which can indicate an over-active immune system. If you suffer from regular colds or infections of any sort, you should mention this to your doctor as there must be an underlying reason. Although homeopathy can be controversial, I believe that it has helped me in the past and could be considered. It may help to remove toxins and long-standing infections from your system gently and naturally. My food intolerances and endometriosis are both autoimmune diseases and so I think that I have a basic problem with my immune system. I mentioned this a few times to my doctors but they did not really investigate it any further, so I decided to research auto-immunity myself and I found that eating the correct foods for me is an essential aspect of managing my autoimmune disorders. Antioxidants are essential for me and so I am taking açaí berry powder, which is a superfood. Other sources of antioxidants include alpha lipoic acid, blueberries, green tea (just not too much if you are trying to conceive – see Chapter 1) and plenty of fresh fruit and vegetables. I have recently discovered that bee pollen may help to build up your immune system and allergy relief. It can also restore energy and stamina (see Chapter 1). However, be aware that bee pollen is not safe to take if you are pregnant or if you have a pollen allergy.

The more I research food and nature, the more convinced I become that God gave us everything we need if we just know where to look for it. Hippocrates said 'Let food be your medicine and medicine be your food.' Thankfully I love my vegetables and am also trying to eat more raw food. Our immune systems are bombarded with all of the additives and pesticides that are in much of our food these days and so our systems can become overloaded and confused. Organic food is, of course, best but, depending upon where you live, it is not always readily available. I have been researching ways of counteracting and eliminating these toxins through supplementing with natural remedies. The liver and kidneys particularly need to be helped as they can get overloaded with toxins leading to problems such as fatigue, sluggishness, head-aches and muscle pain. Burdock helps to eliminate toxins and chicory, milk thistle or dandelion root stimulates and cleanses the liver. Drinking eight glasses of filtered water a day is also essential. Ginseng is excellent for the overall activity of the immune system and Echinacea increases the white blood cell count, which helps the immune system. Speak to the staff in your local health food shop and they can recommend a good combination and dosage of these remedies. However, it is always best to take in nutrients through food rather than supplements so eating the superfoods discussed in Chapter 1 will hopefully strengthen and normalise your immune system and so form a part of the solution to your particular problem.

Dr Alan E. Beer's book, *Is Your Body Baby-Friendly?*, discussed in Chapter 2, goes into great detail about how an over-active immune system can affect fertility and why this happens, and is well worth reading for this aspect alone.

Food Intolerances

Serious food intolerances affect the immune system and allergic reactions can cause the resulting antibodies to attack the foetus or sperm. They also affect your overall vitality and health because you are not able to absorb the nutrients from your food properly. If you suspect you suffer from food intolerances you should get tested and then adjust your diet accordingly and boost your immune system (see previous section on over-active immune systems). You will feel so much healthier and increase your chances of a healthy pregnancy. You can be tested locally by a dietician or nutritionist, which your GP or local health food shop should be able to recommend.

I had my food intolerances tested quite comprehensively by a UK company called Cambridge Nutritional Sciences. They sent me over a test pack, which included all I needed to take a sample of blood and the packaging in which to send it back. I would recommend getting the nurse in your GP practice to take the blood sample for you as this is easier than trying to take it yourself. Once you send off your sample, you get your results back in about ten days and you also receive a booklet with information about suitable diets. The test I did, called

Foodprint 40, is very comprehensive; I also had a test done to check if my yeast levels were too high at the same time.

Yeast

Too much yeast in your system can distort the balance of bacteria in the vagina which is toxic to sperm, thereby interfering with conception. The presence of vaginal yeast infections could indicate that there is too much yeast (candida) in the intestines also, which can affect the absorption of nutrients from our food. If you suffer from recurrent yeast infections you should discuss with your doctor how best to treat this and how it may be affecting your fertility. If you are worried about having excessive yeast in your system, your dietician or nutritionist should be able to test for this.

Cushing Syndrome

Cushing syndrome is a condition where too much cortisol hormone is produced by the adrenal gland, leading to lower sperm production in men and abnormal ovulation in women. Symptoms can include irregular or no menstrual cycles, distinctive fat between the shoulder blades, high blood pressure, obesity and water retention. Other symptoms include acne, abnormal hair growth and a moon-shaped face. It is treated by taking a steroid medication to correct the hormone levels. Once hormone levels have been corrected, and providing there are no other fertility issues, a normal pregnancy should be possible.

Chromosomal Problems

All of the cells in our bodies have chromosomes; they are the building blocks of our body and contain our own unique genetic code. They can be abnormal in three ways: gain in number, loss in number or change in structure. The number of chromosomes in a fertilised egg should be 46 (two pairs of 23 chromosomes, with one of each pair inherited from the mother and the other from the father). Most chromosomal abnormalities can cause serious problems and are lethal, and so the cells carrying them die. For this reason, most embryos carrying chromosome abnormalities die in the first few weeks, and so chromosomal abnormalities are a major cause of miscarriage. If the couple's chromosomes are normal and there are no genetic problems then it is perfectly possible to conceive a healthy baby. Most chromosome abnormalities in miscarriage are caused by the condition of the cells at the time of development of the eggs and sperm. Very rarely do they reflect an inherent problem in one or both members of the couple.

During my research I came across the work of Dr Judy Ford, an internationally respected geneticist who has spent years studying chromosomal abnormalities in miscarriage. She states that these abnormalities occur because one or both members of the couple have been exposed to chemicals, or have a dietary deficiency or a bad habit (such as drinking heavily, smoking, taking drugs or exposing the testes to too much heat). Infections and viruses can also be a problem. However, chromosomal problems can be overcome by correcting poor diet and lifestyle. In order to prevent or reduce the likelihood of chromosomal problems, both you and your partner should take steps to reduce stress in your life, improve your diet and participate in regular gentle exercise. Smoking is an obvious toxin that should be eliminated totally and you also should not consume excessive alcohol.

Male Infertility Issues

There are also a number of problems which men can suffer from that cause infertility. Some of the most common are detailed below.

Sperm Health

Sperm health is determined by *quantity* (over 20 million sperm per millilitre), *quality* (more than 4 per cent should have a normal shape and structure – oval head and long tail) and *motility* (more than 40 per cent should be moving). Daily multivitamins containing Vitamins E and C will help optimal sperm production and function (Wellman Conception is good) and if there are issues maca root or alpha lipoic acid supplements can be beneficial. Eating fresh fruit and vegetables rich in antioxidants will also help. Stress may interfere with the hormones needed to produce sperm and decrease sexual function so, just like their partners, men should try to eliminate or reduce stress in their life. Physical activity is good for reproductive health as well as overall health. However, if men exercise to exhaustion they may experience a temporary change in hormone levels and drop in sperm quality. Men are also most likely to produce high-quality sperm if they maintain a healthy weight. Avoid smoking and drugs and limit alcohol. Spending too much time in hot baths or saunas can also lower the sperm count. Avoid certain medications – anabolic steroids, antibiotics and certain medications used to control chronic conditions such as high blood pressure or inflammatory bowel disease can reduce fertility. If you are on any of these medications you should discuss the issue with your doctor. If there is an issue with your sperm count or motility, don't panic because taking the above measures can often improve things dramatically in as little as three months. Again, check out the superfoods in Chapter 1 as they could offer a simple solution.

A good website with much more detail about sperm evaluation and testing is www.fertility-docs.com.

Retrograde Ejaculation

Retrograde ejaculation causes semen to exit via the bladder instead of the penis during orgasm. It is then flushed out by urination. This condition can be caused by nerve damage, medications, diabetes or surgery which damages the sphincter muscle. It is not a dangerous condition but it does affect fertility and will need treatment in order for a man's partner to conceive. This is the least common ejaculation problem which men may experience.

Varicoceles

Varicoceles are a type of varicose vein that can develop in the scrotum, caused by blood flowing backwards into the testicles and stretching the veins around the testicles. Varicoceles usually occur in younger men and affect approximately 10 per cent of the male population. They can cause no symptoms and are usually harmless. However, sometimes they can cause pain or shrinkage, and reduced sperm production. This can lead to fertility problems and so the varicoceles will need to be treated with surgery.

Blocked Vas Deferens/Epididymal Obstruction

Sperm are produced in the seminiferous tubules within the testes. From there they travel through the tightly coiled epididymis and then the vas deferens to the penis, mixing with semen along the way. A blockage can occur along this passage, preventing sperm from being ejaculated. This blockage could be natural or caused by a hernia or repair of a hydrocele (a build-up of fluid in the scrotum). A blockage on one side can lead to a low sperm count but if there is a blockage on both sides then it is likely that there will be a zero sperm count.

A doctor should be able to feel a blockage during a physical examination. They would then order a testicular biopsy to ensure good sperm is being produced and rule out the presence of other blockages. Surgery can often bypass the blockage. If the obstruction cannot be repaired then sperm can be retrieved from the scrotum and then frozen. The couple can then use this sperm to conceive through IVF or ICSI.

Male Bacterial Infections

Male bacterial infections can be a common cause of infertility. The infection can cause scarring which can cause blockages of tubes and affect sperm production, or the body's immune response to the infection can cause the production of chemical by-products which can be toxic to sperm.

Bacteria can infect the testis (causing orchitis), the epididymis (causing epididymitis) and the prostate (causing prostatitis). All of these conditions affect fertility as sperm production and transport of the sperm are impaired. When an infection occurs, the immune system responds by flooding the area with white blood cells. An excess of white blood cells in the semen can cause damage and affect the sperm's ability to fertilise an egg, and can also cause DNA damage which results in fertilisation failure. The immune system produces antibodies which cause sperm to clump together, also making them useless for fertilisation.

In order to diagnose an infection in the semen, a sample is taken and tested in a laboratory. Depending on the diagnosis, antibiotics can be prescribed to kill the bacteria. If the infection is sufficiently serious to cause scarring and blocked tubes, then surgery is an option to restore fertility. In the worst cases, if the tubes cannot be unblocked, then sperm can be recovered and ICSI, where the sperm are injected into the egg in the uterus, is an option.

Some common bacteria that affect men are found in sexually transmitted diseases (STDs), such as gonorrhoea, syphilis and chlamydia. Both members of a couple should be screened for STDs to ensure neither is infected.

Unexplained Infertility

Here's the thing — unexplained is not good enough in my humble opinion. If your doctor says that they don't know what your problem is, and if you have the energy and resources to carry on, then search for another expert in this field and get that diagnosis. Although it may be difficult to find, there is always a reason. Become your own expert and make sure that you and your partner maintain a healthy lifestyle (mind, body and spirit). Ensure that you are doing everything in Chapter 1 and please also read *Is Your Body Baby-Friendly?* (www.babyfriendlybook.com — discussed in Chapter 2). Dr Alan E. Beer had a very high success rate in treating supposedly unexplained infertility. He connects many infertility problems to the immune system, which all of my issues are connected to, and may help to shed some light on your problems.

Conclusion

Whatever your fertility issue is, or combination of issues as in my case, research and study them and take control of them. Do what you have to do to solve them. The reality is that no matter how nice your doctor or therapist is, and no matter how much they want to help you get your baby, no one cares as much as you and your partner, so you need to be the managers of this situation, employing the expertise and know-how of others, but making your own decisions and being in charge yourselves. I mentioned earlier that I believe that there always has to be a reason and this is true, but I also believe that there is an element of fate or destiny involved. For example, I believe that I will get my baby when I have learned, experienced or done something that I am supposed to do. So, I keep my mind and heart open to what I can learn or do while I am waiting. It's not always easy or, should I say, it is at times incredibly difficult, so I hope that the next chapter of this book will help you to endure the tough days and I wish you every success in overcoming your own hurdles.

4

Emotional Layer Cake

Trying for a baby and constantly failing takes its toll on you. There are so many emotions involved and they only become more complicated the longer it goes on. I have described the sense of failure to my husband as like going for the same job interview month after month and continually being rejected. Can you imagine what this does to your self-confidence? It can be a lonely experience sometimes too. I have tried to remember every negative emotion that I have gone through or that someone else has told me about from their experience. Hopefully, if you need to, you will be able to dip into whichever section resonates with you on any given day for some comfort, and you will know that you are not alone.

Other people around you can be of great support or, through not knowing what to say or do, can make you feel worse. In order to explain some of my emotions, I have used a couple of examples of times when I was feeling low and someone has made me feel worse. This is not to make anyone feel bad if they have said that same thing to me or anyone else, as I would be no expert in what to do if I had not been through this myself. They are merely examples to illustrate a point and to help people understand what to do or say in future.

In order for you to know that I can fully empathise with what you are going through, and so my advice is coming from a place of understanding and experience, I am now going to share my worst time with you. I hope that it will give you hope that you can come back from any trauma if you are determined to do so.

The Worst Three Weeks of My Life

A few years ago, after three years of trying to have a baby, I was pregnant for longer than five weeks. We were happy but tried not to think about it too much while we awaited the ultrasound scan. We had been through enough, in our opinion, at that stage and so absolutely deserved for everything to be ok. Unfortunately, at nine weeks, we experienced the profound and utter misery that is a silent scan. Silence from the ultrasound machine, silence from the doctor and silence from the midwife. I can remember vividly not hearing the heartbeat and being panic-stricken and searching the faces around me for hope. Those faces could hardly look back at me because they were dreading confirming the unbearable news. The saddest three weeks of my life followed. A second scan was scheduled for ten days later and we tried to carry on as normal during that time, hoping that my dates were wrong. Outwardly, I was trying to be positive but looking back now there are many signs that I knew deep down all was lost. Just after the first scan, we went to Old Trafford to see a Manchester United game, which I had booked a few months earlier for Dessie's birthday. We stayed beside the Trafford Centre, which has an amazing selection of shops, but I hardly even looked around (which is totally not like me when it comes to shopping). Then, when we came back, my brother-in-law Paul and his family came for dinner. We hadn't told anybody anything because we had not even announced that we were pregnant and we were still trying to be optimistic. When they were leaving, our niece Kate, who was only about five at the time, said to her parents that she didn't want to leave us because we were sad. They did not know what she meant but it is amazing how children can often see more than adults. Finally, when I was driving to the hospital for the second scan, I met my brother-in-law Marty on the road and he rang my sister Nikki to ask what was wrong with me because I was driving so slowly (I have slowed down a lot but at that time it was not unusual for me to have several points for speeding on my licence). Underneath it all, I obviously knew what we were heading into despite the fact that I was trying to be positive in my head.

The second scan was the same – devastatingly silent. Time stood still for several minutes as the fact that our baby had not survived sank in slowly and then, of course, the practicalities had to be dealt with. So the doctor booked me in for a D&C, scheduled for ten days later. I felt as though I had died myself and walked around the hospital like a ghost, going from one department to another to have bloods taken and I can hardly remember what else, trying to get my head around it. There was one lovely, kind nurse, who realised I needed some space. She took the time to bring me into a room, shut the door, sit down beside me and just let me talk and cry. Of course, Dessie was devastated too. After the initial upset, he just went into minding-me mode. I phoned my mum on the way home from the hospital to ask her to come out to us but couldn't tell her why. You see, I had not told her I was pregnant because this would have been her first grandchild and she would have been so excited; I didn't want to get her hopes up when we had already had some problems. The twelve-week mark would have been on her birthday and we were going to tell her then. God love her, she arrived out to our house and I think I became a little girl again. I just bawled my eyes out and told her our awful news when I was in that terrible traumatised state. I am sorry now that I didn't tell her that I was pregnant earlier. I have never had that experience of telling my mum that I am pregnant and sharing that moment with her. Instead I only have that memory of telling her that I was pregnant but wouldn't be for much longer. Of course, she was devastated too.

For the following ten days, I stayed at home and tried desperately to persuade our little dote back to life. I got up in the morning, showered, dressed, ate nutritiously and lay on the sofa with a hot-water bottle on my tummy. I stupidly (or desperately) thought that if I kept him warm, nourished and still, he might revive. I had a craniosacral therapy session some months later and my therapist told me that the muscles in my womb were still in the holding position – that was obviously the only way that I could hold my baby. Walking into hospital for the D&C, flanked by my husband and my mum, on the day when we should have been sharing our good news at the twelve-week mark, was the hardest thing I have ever had to do. It might seem silly but even though two more scans had confirmed that there was no heartbeat, I felt guilty and grief-stricken at the thought of giving up this little soul I loved so much already. In the three weeks after the first scan, I got closer to my baby than before because all of my thoughts and efforts were with him 24/7. It's strange but you never react to these situations in the way you would expect to before you are in them. A few years before, when I was in my wonderfully naive twenties, a pregnant colleague of mine had discovered that her baby had died. She was left in limbo for a few weeks before a procedure was carried out to induce her. At the time, I wondered how anyone could bear to carry their lifeless baby inside them for so long. However, when my turn came, I did not want to give my baby up.

The experience in hospital was awful. Dessie and Mum came with me so that I wouldn't have to be alone. However, they were left in a waiting room and I was brought off to have a cannula put into my arm. The hospital was very busy that day and this ended up being done in an office because the mortified, but very kind, junior doctor couldn't find another space to do it in. A nurse then took me away and left me sitting on a stool in the public hallway. It was my local hospital so people were walking past me saying hello while I just wanted to crawl into the corner and be invisible. I could see their countenance change when they saw my dead face looking back at them and I didn't have it in me to even try to talk. I didn't kick up a fuss and demand that a nurse bring me back to Dessie because I just did not have the energy. I was concentrating on our baby and saying goodbye to him. I felt as though I had nothing left in me. Another nurse tried to distract me by talking about my sister's wedding but, although I am sure she was trying to be kind, it was the last thing on my mind. I just wanted to be quiet. We had good medical insurance so I was hoping for a private room but there was none. So, I was put into a ward with the curtain pulled around me and given a tablet which was going to make me start to bleed. When that happened a few hours later, I was ready for surgery. My dignity had been stripped from me at the front door. Dessie and Mum were called back in at that stage and stayed with me until I was brought to theatre. The last thing I remember was Dessie kissing me and thinking how much I loved him and that I didn't deserve his love because I was letting him down by not having taken better care of our baby.

I remember coming out of the anaesthetic and just feeling nothing. I was delayed leaving the hospital because my blood pressure dropped very low, but eventually I left later that night. I just wanted to get home. I was very quiet and calm the next day and don't think I even talked much to my family who came to see me. On Saturday, I woke up and heard my sisters Nikki and Emer talking in the kitchen with Dessie. I got up and went out to them. They were chatting and I sat on the sofa and listened for a few minutes. Then all of a sudden I just started to wail like a banshee. It came from the pit of my tummy and must have been awful to hear because I remember looking at their faces and thinking that I had to pull myself together because I was scaring them. The thing is that no matter how much people love you, they don't really understand how you feel unless they have been there themselves. Going through a miscarriage is very tough for husbands and partners as well, but in a different way. They may not have to deal with the hormones and physical pain but they contain a lot of their own feelings while caring for us and they have had their hopes dashed too.

This experience was the most traumatic that I have ever been through and I know that I didn't deal with it head-on when I should have, for various reasons. About a week after my D&C, we discovered that my sister-in-law was pregnant, at the same stage as we were. They deserved this baby (my goddaughter, gorgeous little Mia) so much and I didn't want to spoil their excitement in any way, so I tried to recover too quickly and be 'fine' with it. While I was over the moon for them, I was naturally daunted at the prospect of watching their pregnancy develop and then their child grow up. How was I not going to let this be an ongoing problem? As a result, I became quite rundown physically and it was nine or ten months later before I dealt with my emotions properly. That was when I re-discovered emotional freedom techniques (EFT) through Ronnie Turner in the Turner Clinic in

Stillorgan; this helped me enormously. While I can still cry at the memory of all this if I bring myself back there, I can think about it without trauma, if that makes sense. I had to work hard to find my way back, keep my eyes and heart open to what could help me and stay determined that, whatever happened, I wouldn't lose myself or be beaten by any experience. I believe that you have to come out of these challenges that life throws at you enriched or better in some way, or at least to have learned something. Otherwise, you become less than yourself. Of course, I was also lucky to have the support of my husband and family (Mum, Nikki, Emer, Rachel, Annette, Maureen, Brian, Brian Jnr and Fr Brian), who are all amazing and kind – I love them more than words can say.

Sadly, we have been unfortunate enough to experience a second missed miscarriage. While the silent scan and losing the baby was as sad and devastating as it always is, thankfully the hospital experience was easier in some respects. I feel that I need to mention this so that the importance of proper procedures is recognised. We had a new doctor, who was so understanding without us having to ask for or explain anything, and so we did not have to wait as long for the D&C. His words were genuine and heartfelt, simply 'I am so sorry that you are going through this.' There was also a private room available, which afforded me more dignity in the circumstances. I cried a river for this little soul who did not have a chance at life and can still find myself sighing a lot and shaking my head, as though in disbelief that it had happened again. However, I saw a difference in myself compared to past experiences. I have learned how to deal with many of the other emotional aspects of this particular journey, which you will read about later in this chapter, so my feelings were less complicated. I felt sad but strong and I was not afraid of unravelling. I do not believe in any way that it was easier because I have somehow gotten used to this experience of losing a baby. For me, I have felt different energies with pregnancies, and with this last one I definitely felt the presence of an impish little soul who I was looking forward to having to scold for being as naughty as her father. Our loss was very great. I just knew how to cope better and trusted in my own strength to overcome and get back to myself in due time. As Dessie said, 'Anyway Magoo, this won't beat us' (my maiden name is McGoohan, hence 'Magoo').

Damn Periods

Our monthly period is a pain in the neck at the best of times, but it is also signals our fertility. However, when you are trying to conceive and your period arrives it can feel like your body is betraying you and letting you down. It is devastating because you really wanted to try out that pregnancy test in your bathroom cabinet. Unfortunately, you can't go around like a drama queen crying, 'I've just got my period waaahhh!', which is what you sometimes feel like doing. I remember I was having lunch in my friend's house one day with her and her three lovely kids when I got that first sensation that it was coming. I was late and really positive that this was the month and so, when I got that feeling, I just had to get out of there. I am sure that she was wondering what the hell happened – I went from being happy and chatty to preoccupied and dying to leave within the blink of an eye. I got back to my car and cried my way back into town. I was fine after having a good cry but you can feel so lonely because no one knows or understands how devastated you feel just because you got your period. Some months are harder than others, depending on your expectations, but you just have to allow yourself to have a wee cry if you need to and then look to the month ahead – onwards and upwards!

I Have Had a Miscarriage or Missed Miscarriage

There are no words to describe how awful this is for you. My heart goes out to you and your partner. The pain is unbearable. I am so sorry for your loss. Please do not feel that this is your fault in any way because it is not. It is absolutely not fair that your hopes and dreams have been taken from you and your little soul is not with you anymore. You feel as though a part of you is gone, which it is. You will never forget your little baby and will never want to. One of the toughest parts of this is that not everybody around you will understand your grief. People say things like 'At least you know you can get pregnant' or 'Sure you can try again', and they are really trying to be kind and motivating in some way. However, these words hurt because they don't understand and acknowledge the depth of your grief and the fact that this baby will never be replaced, no matter how many babies you have. When we lose a baby, we may not have ever seen their little face, but we have been imagining it since we got our positive test result. We are grieving for lost dreams and for a little soul who didn't get even a chance at a future. There is nothing to be done but take some time out to cry and think and talk and cry some more. This too shall pass, even if you feel like you don't want to ever let go of your grief or your baby.

When you are ready, you will breathe, get up in the morning, shower, eat, go to work and basically just function. You must, however, look after yourself because you have been through a draining experience, both physically and emotionally. Make sure that you don't get run down. I know that you probably don't care about this right now, but when you are physically healthy, everything is just a little bit easier to bear. Vitamin B complex is good for stress so it would be good to take some supplements. Vitamin C and zinc are also good for healing.

It can be comforting to do something to remember your baby. I planted a tree once for a lost baby and it makes me smile every spring when it blossoms. It's a white cherry blossom and I don't think that I realised its symbolism when I planted it – it blossoms for such a short time. There is also a service of remembrance every year, organised by the Miscarriage Association of Ireland, for babies lost through miscarriage. Even if you can't attend it, you could go to Mass in your own church, or even light a candle, on the same day to remember your little soul. It can also be very healing to do something in memory of your child, so that in your pain you are helping someone else, such as donating money to Temple Street Children's University Hospital (www.cuh.ie), Our Lady's Children's Hospital, Crumlin (www.olchc.ie) or Pomegranate (www.pomegranate.ie), an organisation that provides financial aid to couples going through IVF.

You definitely need someone to talk to, so if there is no one who you can talk freely to and who understands, then please avail of the counselling services that your hospital should let you know about. By burying your pain, all you will do is prolong the agony because it will still be there, buried deep, until such a time as you deal with it.

I have mentioned in Chapter 3 that I hate the term 'missed miscarriage'. It makes it sound like something you meant to do but somehow forgot. It does not describe or do justice to what has actually happened. Your baby has died and must now be taken from you by surgery. This is not fair and you don't deserve this. You need to take some time out to deal with what has happened and you and your partner need to look after each other. Then, when you are ready, you will come back to life and try again.

The Miscarriage Association of Ireland (www.miscarriage.ie) and the UK Miscarriage Association (www.miscarriageassociation.org.uk) can help. While you will never forget your baby, you can come out of this stronger and the sun will shine again, I promise.

Why Has This Happened to Me – Don't I Deserve a Baby?

Anyone who wants a baby as much as you do deserves to have one. Life is great, but it is not easy or fair. The sooner you accept this fact the sooner you can move on, take control and deal with it. Believe it or not, this is not personal. We are merely small specks in the universe and every single one of us has some cross to bear. This just happens to be ours. We may not be in control of what cross we are given but we are certainly in control of how we deal with it. Suit up and take control by educating yourself and learning about your own individual fertility. This will help you to make good choices about what to do and give you the best possible chance for success. Of course you deserve a baby. This fact alone, unfortunately, just doesn't guarantee that you will get one easily.

Everyone Around Me Is Getting Pregnant and It's Hard to Deal With – Am I a Bad Person?

No, you are not at all bad, merely human. Of course it is difficult to see others around you with growing bellies when that is all you want. You are just thinking, 'Why can't I experience that?' This does not take away from your happiness for them. It is absolutely possible to be happy for someone else and sad for yourself at the same time. It is also much better to acknowledge your feelings to someone close and just get it off your chest; this will help to lift your frustration. Think to yourself, 'I will be happy for them because I know that they will be happy for me when I am pregnant', even though this can be difficult to do in practice.

My Friend's Baby Is Due When Mine Should Have Been

When you have suffered miscarriages, or even have just been trying to conceive unsuccessfully for a while, it is natural to feel a pang when you hear about other women's joy at being pregnant if they are in your circle, as you will be confronted with their pregnancy on a regular basis. This has nothing to do with how happy you are for them and doesn't make you a bad person – merely human. As I said before, it is perfectly possible to feel happy for someone else and sad for yourself at the same time. I repeat this because it took a while for this to sink in with me and so I didn't acknowledge my feelings about how I felt for myself and ended up stressed because of my conflicting emotions. I have been through this situation a few times and it can sometimes be tough. However, how hard it is depends on your friend. I have found some harder than others. This is especially true if there is no acknowledgement from the other person of what you might be feeling, when they know exactly what you have been through.

When my sister was pregnant, she kept me involved and included but never once mentioned the heartbeat because she knew about my awful experiences with silent scans. She checked in with me regularly to ask if I found any aspect particularly tough to deal with. Because of this, I had no problem with her pregnancy because she respected my feelings without making me feel like she was walking on eggshells around me.

The thing is, you cannot demand any particular consideration, merely hope for some. You certainly do not want it to be all about you but some small acknowledgement or consideration is very much appreciated. All you can do is make sure that if their pregnancy is on the harder end of the scale you look after yourself. Do what you can handle and no more. If you don't feel like sitting in on a conversation about how tired they feel or how hard it is, then don't. If there is a specific event which you feel like you could not handle attending, such as a baby shower or Christening, you should not feel like you have to go, and your friend should understand your decision and realise that this is not a slight on them. Make sure you have someone to vent to and just get any frustration off your chest and out of your system. Remember that additional stress could hinder your chances so do what you have to do to deal with the situation. Emotional freedom techniques (EFT) and meditation always make me feel more grounded and like a better person. If neither of these attract you, then perhaps some other form of exercise would be good. Experiment and find what works for you. If she is truly a friend she will understand and be your shoulder to cry on if you need to.

When the baby is born, if your friend just doesn't know how to handle the situation, then go to see the baby, do your duty and be nice, and then go home and cry. It can be devastating to see a newborn when you should be having your baby too. My arms are going around you now if you are in this situation. The pain of your loss is excruciating. I remember having a mini panic attack (which is not like me – I'm a placid Taurus) when someone brought their newborn to our house to meet other people. For some reason, it was more than I could bear to have people welcoming and cooing over this baby for the first time in my own home, when I should have been showing off mine. I had to stay in the bathroom until I could compose myself and then went out and did my best. You would imagine that people would consider your feelings in these situations but the truth is that most of the time people aren't actually thinking about you and are just excited and living in their own bubble; it isn't personal. Think about what you have already been through and you will realise how strong you actually are. You can deal with this; just remember to breathe and breathe again and this too shall pass.

Where Has My Self-Confidence Gone?

I have thought about this a lot and I have come to the conclusion that one of the main reasons why we lose our self-confidence when something traumatic happens to us is because we suddenly realise that we are not in control of every aspect of our lives. I have certainly gone through this myself, and have also seen family and friends who have been bereaved or had something else terrible happen to them go through this. When we experience a shock, which changes the direction of our lives irrevocably, we become uncertain and confused as to what to do next. I believe that it is also true that in most cases we fight against what we don't want to accept or understand and so this makes it even harder to move in any direction.

Another reason, of course, is that our fertility is at the very core of our identities. Even when we are little girls, we play with dolls and practice our nurturing and caring. We believe that having a baby is one of the reasons why we are here and an entitlement if we so wish. Infertility can make us question our very existence.

Acceptance of our situation is the key to taking back control of our lives. This isn't always an easy thing to do. However, if we accept our situation, we can actually look it in the face, deal with it and decide what to do about it and what our new direction will be. Even though we may not be in control of what has happened, we are certainly in control of how we carry on and this can return our sense of control or confidence in ourselves. It amazes me the strength with which people deal with all sorts of traumas and tragedies in their lives every day of the week. Getting up in the morning can be a Trojan effort when you have suffered a loss. I believe that we don't give ourselves enough credit for how strong we are when we actually get through our day, even though we are feeling utterly destroyed. If you can acknowledge just how strong you are being in just carrying on, you can see that you will be able to get back to yourself.

Acceptance of a bad situation is not always easy or palatable. However, having fought against it on several occasions, I can honestly say that acceptance is the best way to move forward, find your way back to yourself and regain your inner confidence.

Nobody Talks About It

Apart from the obvious pain of not yet having held our baby in my arms, I have found that there are several other layers of stress to this problem that really could be relieved if people didn't feel so awkward about this subject. Being challenged in the fertility department is horrible enough, but especially so because people generally don't acknowledge it. It's bad enough to not only have to go through this, but to become a person who makes people feel awkward through no fault of your own is very upsetting. I have never had a problem talking about what was going on if anyone ever asked me, but very few actually did, apart from my own family and only a couple of friends. I tended not to bring it up because politeness dictates that you don't want to spoil someone's day with your problems. I don't feel at all ashamed about our fertility problems but apparently some people do. There is no need for shame or embarrassment and there is a huge need for people to support you. One day, someone asked me why I stick to my rigid diet so fastidiously. I explained that it was linked to my endometriosis and it may help to control it. Their face changed and they stopped talking and went all quiet. Again, I would have been happy to explain some more about it, but their whole body language told me to stop and I felt bad. It is hard to explain, but if I had said that my diet would help my coeliac disease I am sure that we would have had a long discussion about other people's experiences with this and advice would have been given, and so on. Once it is fertility related, it is somehow off-bounds for a lot of people. I realise that this reaction can stem from some sort of politeness around the subject but I would like to let people know that if someone is open to talking about their fertility-related conditions, it is perfectly polite and supportive to do so. For several years, I over-compensated when I thought someone was feeling awkward, and I still would in the company of people who are acquaintances rather than close friends and family. I certainly do not expect, and would not want, everyone I meet in my daily life to talk about my fertility, although it is amazing how many people feel no awkwardness about demanding to know when you will have children when you get married first. However, people who are in your life and whom you consider family and friends should take an interest in what is going on with you, and if they care about you they will realise when you need to talk about your situation.

The media occasionally cover stories about couples who have been successful with IVF but there are very few examples of people who are bang in the middle of this heartache and limbo. The only television show that I ever saw which covered a couple in the middle of fertility treatments was *Giuliana and Bill* on the Style Network in the United States. This is a reality show that followed two celebrities who got married and then decided to try for a baby. When they discovered that they were facing fertility challenges, they could have decided not to include it in their show but I am truly grateful that they were brave enough to talk about and share their story. They had the exact same conversations that Dessie and I had, and I became glued to their story because watching them made me feel less alone. It turns out that I am not batty because Giuliana had exactly the same insecurities as I had. Bill reminded me so much of my Dessie in the way he looked after his wife and said all the right things. During the show, Giuliana was diagnosed with breast cancer. She had a double mastectomy and I admire her courage so much for doing this. Because of her cancer treatment, she will not be able to get pregnant for a few years but they now have a baby through the help of a surrogate. I am not a huge fan of reality shows but I was glued to their story and am so thrilled that they now have the baby they dreamed of after going through so much.

To get back to the point, there is very little in the media that you can relate to and very few people may be comfortable talking to you about it so I would recommend looking up an organisation called the National Infertility Support and Information Group (www.nisig.ie). It organises support groups in Dublin and Cork and publishes quarterly newsletters, and this could be a good place to start. Support groups and blogs are fantastic but I still think that, as humans, we all want the people in our lives and our peers to understand us. Hopefully, this book will help.

Why Does Nobody Ask Us About What We Are Going Through?

For some reason, the subject of fertility is taboo in most circles. I would love it if people outside of my own family and friends asked me more about the issue because I think that we can only break the taboo if people talk about it. There is some contradiction in the fact that people seem to feel awkward about our situation and yet have no hesitation in bombarding us with stories of their or other people's pregnancies and babies. I have heard other people say 'Oh she doesn't talk about it' but the fact is that if someone says to you 'How are you?' we all say 'Great, thanks.' It's a pleasantry and the response is a reflection of that. If someone asks me a direct question about fertility or babies, I have no problem in talking about it. I mean, how hard is it to say 'How are you coping?' or 'Is this situation hard for you?' We can only be grateful that people are interested in how we are doing. Of course, I am talking about people in our own circle. I think that sometimes people are afraid of bringing up a subject in case it is painful for us but, if we are living with it, then it is on our mind anyway.

Who Can We Ask for Support?

Accept the fact that the people who love you will be there for you and will ask you how you are coping and if they can help. I have also found that you will receive support, help and guidance on occasion from 'angels' who suddenly appear in your life at exactly the right moment and are gone again before you know it. However, if you try to force the issue with some people, they will only get awkward and this makes you feel worse. Try to take the support from wherever you get it and don't spend too much time worrying about where you are not getting it from. Organisations and support groups can help, like the National Infertility Support and Information Group (www.nisig.ie). Infertility is just one of many challenges that face people in life. Into every life a little rain shall fall, but life is all about how you deal with the crosses each of us has to bear.

Other People's Expectations, Comments and Insensitivities

Again, I must note that any examples I use here are meant only to illustrate a point and help you in the future, not to make anyone feel bad if they didn't know what to say or do in a certain situation in the past – I am not perfect either, believe it or not.

When we got married first and started trying for a baby, I loved the expectations and talk of the pitter patter of tiny feet and being teased about not drinking. However, when it started to dawn on me that things were not going to be that easy, it was tough when people passed comments. I would smile, but it made my tummy twist painfully inside me. It was worse however when they stopped directing these comments towards me and started directing them towards others instead. I felt as though they had given up on me, which might sound strange or over-sensitive, but it is a sensitive subject. I remember being mortified at a baby shower one time when people were saying 'oh you'll be next' to a woman who was only just engaged while I was sitting nearby and had been married for a couple of years. I carried on as normal, talking and laughing, but I felt awful inside. The one that really still gets me though is when Dessie is holding a baby and someone says 'It really suits you.' He is a gentle giant and babies are very calm with him. This brings back my feelings of guilt about the fact that I haven't given him his own baby.

Some women (and it is mostly women) seem to feel like you are to be pitied if you do not have children and have no qualms about displaying this. Have you ever been asked by someone you haven't seen of a long time 'So have you any kids?' and when you say 'No', they say 'And when did you get married?' Their face then turns into a calculator, working out how many years that is and then their head tilts to the side and they let out an 'Ahh' and their face turns into an LED display with the words 'She must be having trouble' all over it. Some women go on and on about every other pregnancy in the world to you without even acknowledging that maybe you have a problem because you have been married for a few years, obviously love children and don't have any yet yourself, to the point where you think that they either hate you or at least pity you for being – that awful word – 'childless', because your life must be pointless. I used to let this bother me until one day I looked around me and the light bulb clicked above my head. All sorts of people have babies. I realised that actually having children doesn't define who you are in the eyes of those who truly love you and you will not be judged on this at the end of your days either. I love this quote from an amazing man called Stephen Covey:

'Our ultimate freedom is the power to decide how anybody or anything outside ourselves will affect us.'

Someone else's comment can only bother you if you let it. Most people don't even mean to make you feel bad anyway; they are only just looking for something to talk about.

Have you ever noticed how other people always seem to be thinking about the next stage of your life? When you are going out with someone, it's about getting engaged, when you get engaged it's about the wedding, when you get married it's about having babies, etc. I say we should all just live in the now. I am sure that people make these comments for the sake of conversation, but when you are going through a rough time, it can make you feel as though you are being judged somehow. I am not saying that I would have been any different if things had not been so difficult for us, by the way. I am certainly not perfect and am as capable as the next person of putting my foot in it. However, I certainly know now that none of us should say anything to anyone else that implies that their lives are in any way lacking just the way they are. Find something else to talk about people! I mean, there's always the weather.

I also realised that I am a happy person and it was only the constant failure that upset me. I think that I am actually quite simple because even just the smell of freshly cut grass, a walk in the countryside with Dessie and the dogs (Sky and Barney) or just having a laugh at home around our kitchen table is enough to make me happy. So I decided to acknowledge that my life is great and will continue to be so whether we are blessed with children or not – it's just rather annoying to feel like you have to prove this to people. At the same time, I know that until we come to the end of this particular chapter in our lives (i.e. we either have a baby or decide that the time is right to stop trying), I will possibly have some sad days and shed some more tears. Acceptance of yourself just the way you are is a great thing, although this can take some work. Once you accept yourself totally, nothing anyone else says can touch you.

I Feel so Desperate

Desperation is an awfully toxic emotion and I have felt this in the pit of my stomach at times. I have had times when I did not know how I would survive if I was not pregnant by a certain time or occasion. However, I always did survive. My deadlines came and went and I survived. One fact I am sure about is, and read this slowly and carefully, we – *never* – make – good – decisions – during – desperate – moments. Desperation makes you feel you need to do something – anything – and so you might make decisions about treatments or whatever too quickly because you just need to do *something*, instead of waiting until you are calm and have all the facts, thus optimising your chances of success. It also makes you react to situations in a way that you might not otherwise. For example, I remember crying if I was ovulating and either Dessie or I had to go to a stag or hen party, say, and we couldn't be together. I would desperately think 'What if this was the month and how can I bear to wait another one until I ovulate again?' (By the way, if you can't be together on your day of ovulation, I know now that you just need to get busy the whole week beforehand because sperm can survive for up to five days in the womb so all is not lost!) This might seem silly to an outsider but, when you feel like you are running out of time and grieving, it is often impossible to be rational.

When this feeling comes over you, you need to be by yourself and take some deep breaths and calm down because, remember, we *never* make good decisions during desperate moments.

I found after a while that when this desperation came over me, sometimes praying helped. Now I don't know if I am what you would call religious. I like going into a quiet church and lighting a candle. Saying a prayer meant that I was handing things over to God for a while so I could relax. Meditation is good for calming down too or a yoga class. Other times, going for a walk with the dogs was great, just being in nature. I haven't actually tried hugging a tree but I am open to all sorts! For you, it might be an exercise class or going for a run. Whatever your thing is, do it. Do not succumb to desperation. Take charge and actively do something distracting, or that requires effort, to shake it off. It's not attractive and it will get you nowhere.

My Relationships Are Changing

Changing relationships are inevitable as life goes on. I have sometimes thought that some of mine changed because of my fertility problems but now I can see that this isn't really true. Sure enough, the nature of some of my relationships has changed because of circumstances. For instance, I may not be in contact with some of my friends as often as before, but, in fairness, if they have small children, I am not going to be the first person they call for advice when the children are sick or they are figuring out what crèche or school is good or any of the hundreds of details that must consume parents. They also don't want to call me on their bad days to complain about how difficult parenting is, as they may be afraid that from my perspective this can look like they are ungrateful for having children. Although I understand that bringing up a family is very difficult and would never regard someone as being ungrateful for naturally being frustrated at times, it can create a divide. This does not mean that I don't consider them my friends any more. I don't have to see someone all of the time to consider them friends. Remember also that while you are consumed with this – your particular issue – others have their own problems. I try my best to be aware of when my friends need me but know that there have been times when I was too upset to deal with anything other than getting myself through my own personal problems.

The key point is to go easy on your friends. The nature of your relationship may change but the basis of your friendship does not. I have been able to reconcile a lot of what may have felt like estrangement on occasion (this word is too dramatic but it's the closest I can think of to what I mean) when I think about it this way. You need to learn a few tricks as well. I have two friends with children and I used to meet both of them for lunch together. Much as I love them both, it was awful because they ended up talking to each other about their children and I ended up feeling like the spare wheel. Initially I thought that it was the constant talk about their children that bothered me but then I realised that I had no problem talking to either of them on their own about their children, so it was the feeling of being left out of the conversation that bothered me. The solution was simple – meet them separately.

Those relationships that appear to have faded would probably have done so, regardless of your fertility problems, and it can be a comfort to understand that sometimes people are just in our lives at certain times for a particular reason. With true friends you can always pick up where you left off anyway, no matter how long it is since you spoke to them.

I don't believe that fertility problems are the cause of any problem in our lives other than the obvious one, although it is easy to feel like they affect everything. Throughout this torturous experience you may feel that you have lost some people along the way but you will also receive support from other expected and unexpected sources and start new friendships too. Appreciating this support, wherever it comes from, will fill your heart with warmth, so you should try your best to focus on that.

If We Don't Have a Baby, Will My Husband Be Sorry He Married Me?

Don't be so silly, it's probably just tearing him apart to see what you are going through. Of course, if he really wants children he naturally will wish that things were different, just like you do, but if he loves you enough to marry you and is supporting you through this ordeal, he will know that he would rather spend his life with the woman he loves without children than with a woman he doesn't love with them. Hopefully, you will get your baby. If you don't, life will not end. It will just mean that you can focus more on looking after each other and making each other happy (and have lots more holidays).

Don't stress yourself out about this one. He will only regret it if he loses the woman he married, so you must not lose the sense of yourself in all of this. Find whatever tools you need to stay sane and grounded. I have mentioned emotional freedom techniques (EFT), yoga and meditation before but even just going for a long walk in a beautiful place is good for the soul. I have gone through times when I thought I could never recover, but I worked hard and I did, because I wanted to see the happiness and relief on Dessie's face when I was back to myself. Don't let this challenge beat you or ruin your lovely relationship. It's all about you and him in the end.

How Do I Ensure that My Relationship Doesn't Suffer?

You are both in this together but you need to make sure that you are completely honest with each other about how you feel about everything that happens. For example, in the beginning, I felt guilty that the problem was me. Before all the tests, Dessie used to always say that it was probably him, because he is so nice and loves me so much and didn't want me to feel bad. When we found out that he has super sperm and the problem lay with my physical challenges I felt guilty beyond belief because I know he would be such a super dad. We talked about this a lot for a while and he convinced me that there was nothing to feel bad about because it was just the way things were. I now accept that he will never resent me (although I still feel sick when someone tells him it suits him when he is holding a baby, if I am totally honest) and we talk about everything so I never have to wonder what he is feeling. You also need to make time for each other and, for God's sake, don't make your partner feel like a sperm donor. Of course you are going to concentrate your efforts around the time of ovulation, but let him know that you fancy him all of the time and have fun with each other (if you know what I mean) during the rest of the month too. This is good for both of you. When a man really loves you, it is easy to make him happy. You just need to remember to let him know that you love him back. Make sure you have date nights that are just about the two of you. Little things are important. Our song is Hootie & the Blowfish's 'Only Wanna Be with You'. Every time I hear it on the radio or play the CD I ring Dessie and blare it down the phone at him. It's not always convenient for him when he is on a site and trying to shout instructions at people over bad weather and rain, but it's one of my ways of making sure he knows I love him, even if he is at the other end of the phone saying 'For God's sake Magoo!' to me. At the end of the day, babies or no babies, it's about the two of you being happy with each other for a very long time, so make sure you are having fun.

How Hard Are Fertility Drugs?

The very first time I was prescribed a fertility drug, my doctor looked at my husband, winked as he was writing the prescription, and joked about how they might make me cranky. I probably laughed at this at the time too but, in hindsight, he was actually very patronising and showed that he had no real understanding about the fact that his patients have to carry on living their lives while feeling completely altered and unlike themselves. Feeling 'cranky' is nothing to joke about and however hard he might have thought it would be on my husband, it was ten times harder on me.

I'm not going to lie to you, being on fertility drugs, especially long term, is really tough. I was on them a couple of times and once for over a year and experienced both physical and emotional side effects. My uncle Brian is my father figure and for some reason I used to burst out crying every time he called in to see me. God love him; I am pretty sure he was relieved when I rang him to tell him I was off the fertility drugs, although he didn't admit it he did laugh when I suggested this. When you are trying for a baby, you will take anything that is prescribed to you gladly. However, at no time was I ever given any advice about how to handle being on these drugs, which would have helped. As I became aware of the impact they were having on me emotionally, I learned how to manage the side effects by ensuring my blood sugars were balanced through my diet and avoiding upsetting situations. Meditation is good too if you can find some quiet time.

You must, however, keep your doctor up to date on whatever physical and emotional side effects you are experiencing. I was on a drug that contained cortisol last year and it did not agree with me. I put up with it for several months thinking that I would do anything, regardless of how I felt, if it meant getting our baby. However, after a few months, I actually read the small print on all of my drug boxes. I identified that it was this particular drug that was making me feel so negative and contacted my doctor. He told me to stop taking it and confirmed that it wasn't going to affect my hormone levels. This was a huge relief. Then, after my last laparoscopy, I experienced a lot of bleeding on a particular drug for a few months and so decided myself to stop taking it and talked to my doctor about it at my next appointment. Trust your own instincts and they will tell you if something isn't right; then talk to your doctor. They need to know how these drugs are affecting you. Some of the side effects can be helped with natural remedies like slippery elm and ginger root (just boil in water to make a delicious tea), which will help counteract the irritating effects on the stomach that synthetic drugs can have. Monitor your overall health and trust your own instincts. Keep your eye on the prize as they say and if the side effects are not harming you in other ways but are having the right impact on your hormone levels just keep thinking that you won't be feeling like this forever. However, it is my own opinion, having been on fertility drugs for approximately two years in total, that if the drugs don't work within six months they are not going to and there is another issue to be uncovered and dealt with. I am not a doctor but I am speaking from my own experience and from that of several other women I have spoken to all over Ireland during my travels with Maybe Baby.

How Long Do We Keep Trying?

Unfortunately, there is no straight answer to this one. You and your partner will need to sit down at some point and have a frank discussion about how long you want to give your life over to this. The goal posts may move, as they have for us on several occasions.

During one of my bad days, someone asked me if I could live with myself if I stopped trying. This was such a dramatic thing to say and I was so hurt I don't even know what I said in reply. That person knew all that we had been through but implied that I should keep putting myself through physical and emotional trauma and disappointment. I felt judged for having a weak moment. However, what really hurt me was that, to my ears, they were telling me that unless I had a baby I was less of a person. I had to keep going, no matter what, because I wasn't complete without making this happen. I am delighted to tell you that I am a complete person and will be no less of a person if I don't have a baby.

Getting back to the question, there are of course other factors involved, like money and age. Be open and honest with each other. Do what you can and make sure that you are making decisions based on what you really want and not what you are being pressured into. If you want to go to the ends of the earth or if you think it's time to stop, then you do that and don't let anybody else's opinion get in your way. Remember – you are in control of your own lives and you are the only ones who have to live with your decisions.

Why Should We Keep Going?

There is only one reason to keep going and that is because you both want to and feel that you can emotionally, financially and physically.

Am I Too Old?

I met a very young-looking and full-of-life 40-year-old recently who was told by her GP that she was too old to have a baby. I'm sorry, but the higher powers of nature and/or God (supporting all belief systems, as I do) decide that we are too old to have babies once we have begun menopause, so if this hasn't happened to you yet then don't let anyone tell you or make you feel that you are too old. It is absolutely up to you. One thing that I am conscious of is making sure that I stay fit and energetic so that, if we are so blessed, I will be able to run around and play with our child, and the sleepless nights won't totally wipe me out. With that in mind, my health regime is now a lifestyle choice and not just about conceiving. I want to be fit to enjoy my life no matter what way it turns out. Staying young at heart is also a blessing so try not to get too jaded with the whole experience and remember to smell those lovely flowers and wonder at that beautiful rainbow that God (and/or nature of course) provides for us.

Money Is Holding Us Back

This is, of course, very possibly a problem for many couples in the 'current economic climate' (much as I hate that phrase). Apart from money possibly being an issue for couples who need fertility treatment, there are even perfectly fertile couples who believe that they can't afford to have a baby due to the huge costs of mortgages and childcare. First of all, I would say that just because something isn't possible this week or next week does not mean that you shouldn't be working towards your goal. It can be an interesting exercise to analyse where your money goes on a monthly basis and then determine if there are areas in which you can spend less. For example, you could bring your lunch to work and put the money you save into a deposit account. There is an old saying that if you mind the pennies, the pounds will mind themselves. Just start somewhere and do something, no matter how small, with your goal in mind. The following are things that you can do which don't cost much, or indeed anything at all, and which will help you to be ready for success as soon as things improve (which they always do):

- Eat well – good organic food may be a bit more expensive but if you take the bad things (with no nutritional value) off your shopping list, you will be freeing up some euros to invest in your future. Now, I don't mean that you should go without treats at all. Following my particularly tough food intolerance test, I had to come up with some recipes for my own treats like gluten-free flapjack and seed bars. I also found a dark chocolate bar which has no gluten or dairy, Aine's Lime Dark Chocolate (made in Cavan – on my doorstep), which I am obsessed with. Dark chocolate contains antioxidants so it is good for you as well as delicious.

- Take a regular walk – this is fantastic for the body and the mind. If you go with your partner or your friends you can also have a laugh along the way.
- If you can't afford to go to a class, buy a yoga or meditation CD and book from your local bookshop, or borrow them from your local library, and start practicing. Both of these have really beneficial effects on your health and stress levels.
- Sit down and take a good look at your finances – if you need to, talk to MABS (the Money Advice and Budgeting Service, www.mabs.ie) to help you plan your way to less cash stress in your life. MABS can help you to approach your financial institutions to re-structure loans and mortgages and to develop realistic budgets. Of course, these days there are no guarantees that this will work but you won't know unless you try and it won't cost you a penny to do so.
- If you are in a position to afford the baby when it comes, but need fertility treatment and can't afford that, then look into a charity called Pomegranate (www.pomegranate.ie). You could also help fundraise for this organisation, which provides money to help couples pay for fertility treatment and, you never know, maybe it would be in a position to help you.
- Sit down together and decide what you really want out of your life – maybe you are stressing out in a job you don't like or travelling too much or living somewhere you don't want to be. Forget about what your obstacles are and write down what your ideal goal is. If you can't figure out for yourself how to get there, then read Stephen Covey's *The 7 Habits of Highly Effective People*. You never know what you could learn about yourself that will help you to realise your dream of the life that is perfect for you.
- Laugh – this is very important and free.

- Dance – very important and also free.
- Love – most important of all and thankfully free.
- Believe – anything is possible, look at other times in your life when you realised an ambition or dream that seemed unlikely. Take out a book from your local library about an inspirational character who made things happen for themselves against all odds. Things always get better and with some clear thinking and effort, despite 'austerity' measures, you will find your way and you will find the money you need.
- Have patience – this is hard to come by sometimes but very necessary while you are waiting. This is where the yoga and meditation come in handy. You can also bide your time improving yourself so that you will be an even better parent when the time comes. Join your local library and teach yourself from the amazing store of knowledge contained within: nutrition, baking, sewing, car mainte- nance, languages, etc. The world really is your oyster when you look around outside of yourself and your obstacles.
- Count your blessings – I say my prayers every morning and thank God for all of the good things in my life. As I became more grateful, my list became longer because my eyes were opening to the good and not focusing solely on my losses.

Can We Take a Break from Trying?

Of course you can. Why wouldn't you? It is actually a good idea to take a break, gather yourselves and relieve the pres- sure. You must always listen to your own gut instinct and if you feel the need to stop for a while to build back up your reserves of sanity and health then that is exactly what you should do.

Am I Wasting My Life with this Obsession?

You are never wasting time when you are striving honestly to reach a goal. There are no guarantees with fertility, even if you attend the most qualified and acclaimed specialist in the world. So, while you are doing everything that you can to get your baby, you must have other things going on in your life so that when you look back you will never think that this time was wasted. In our lives, for example, Dessie went back to college part-time and got his degree. I have been building a business with my sister and have also gone back to college. Learn something and improve yourself along the way and the time will not be wasted. Obviously, there have been times when we have had to take time out to heal after disappointments and grief, but we have always tried to keep a perspective on things. At the end of the day, we all have to do things that we are compelled to do and see where that brings us. Hopefully you will be successful but you will also know if you reach a stage where you want to change your direction. Trust yourself and your gut instincts.

What if We Never Have a Baby?

You know what, there are no guarantees and nobody can promise you success. However, if you have not been told at this point that there is no hope, why would you not be as positive as possible? Impossible things happen every day. If the worst-case scenario happens, having worried and fretted about it will not make it any easier when the time comes. Worry and stress will make you ill but being happy and posi-tive can only help you to achieve your goal. Be positive and keep your mind and heart open to what can help you. Give yourself the best chance of winning and enjoy today. Don't forget that life is short and occasionally you have to make lemonade out of lemons.

I realise that you can't just decide to be positive and it will happen overnight. I am blessed with an optimistic nature and even I have had times when I have struggled with this. However, you can start off by deciding that you *want* to be positive. Try to give yourself a break from thinking about your problems. In my experience, once I focused on wanting to be positive, I stopped looking inside and began to try changing things outside of myself that would help me. I always start by making sure my diet is good and my blood sugars are balanced. The next step is spending time with people who love you whether you are up or down and value your company either way. Also, spend time with funny people or watch funny shows on television. Slowly, get outside of yourself and see the lighter side of life. Then, when you are built up and feeling more positive, you can look at your problems again from a new perspective and be more open to seeing what action you can take. If you find that you cannot get yourself out of a negative frame of mind, then I really would recommend talking to a professional counsellor. Life is too short to feel awful if there is help out there, and there is always help, if you just decide to take it.

I Want to Give Up

If you want to give up, then that is exactly what you do. Life is short and who wants to waste it being miserable? We have discussed the possibility that we may not succeed and, while we are still trying, we are not afraid of a future without children. No matter how it feels or what other people think, it is actually not the end of the world if you don't have a baby. In fact, it leaves you free! Free to spend your money on what you want, free to travel wherever you want and free to spend your time how you want. There are many examples of great people who contributed to the world and didn't have children, and likewise there are examples of people for whom having a family didn't make them happy. Like I said in Chapter 1, if you are not well rounded and happy before you have children, you certainly won't be after you have them.

Decide if you are ready to give up and, if you are, you should go for it and celebrate it. No more fertility drugs, no more crushing disappointments. Then, plan a list of things that you would like to experience and do, that you would never have been able to do if you had a family. We have decided that if we are unsuccessful and decide it is time to stop, we will head off on a fabulous holiday across America where we will buy that old Mustang or Jaguar we are always talking about (we are avid fans of Wayne Carini's *Chasing Classic Cars* on Dave) and drive Route 66, and then take it from there. We might even go and live somewhere sunny. Because of my strict diet, we haven't even taken many holidays in the last couple of years. The world is our oyster. Just because life ends up different to how we had planned, doesn't mean that it is worse. The proverb 'be careful what you wish for' is a warning for a reason. Believe that God or life still has something wonderful planned for you and be open to experiencing it. Make sure that you are reconciled with your decision (counselling can help if you need it) and are fully behind it, and then go for life! Do not let this experience lessen you in any way. Let it make you stronger and wiser and ultimately more at peace with yourself.

We Have Been Told that I Can't Have a Baby and I Can't Accept It

So you have been told that there is no hope. This is truly traumatic and I am so sorry for your loss. This is shocking and horrible and so difficult to come to terms with. Surely it is every woman's right to become a mother if she wants to. This news affects your self-confidence and crushes your hopes and dreams for the future. It is not fair that you are in this position but life is not always fair. You just have to turn on the news to know this. You have done nothing to deserve this; it is just the way it is. Everyone gets some cross to bear during their lives and this just happens to be yours. You should take some time out to absorb what this means for you and decide what you need to do to reach some degree of acceptance. I mentioned earlier that I believe acceptance is a gift. You did not choose this but you can decide if it will destroy you or make you stronger. Counselling would be a good idea. You do not want this pain to come back to haunt you at some later stage in your life because you have not dealt with it now. My heart goes out to you.

When you have come to terms with this news, there are other options open to you so this does not have to be the end of your dream of parenthood. Because you have been medically diagnosed, you can begin the process of adoption. This can be a long process so the sooner you start the better. Adoption is an amazing thing to do and you and your partner could be great parents to a very lucky little boy or girl who would bring you so much joy and happiness, if you decide to go this route.

If all options are gone for you, while it is traumatic and awful and desperately unfair because it is something that you really want, this is still not the end of your life. You must learn how to face up to it and deal with it, difficult as that may be. When you are ready, take control of this and accept and embrace the new direction that your life has taken. Do not torment yourself over what might have been when there are still wonderful life experiences out there for you, if you can just open your heart to them. Like I said in the last section, do things that you would never have been able to do if you had kids. The world is your oyster and you can be happy again, if you decide that you want to be and do the work to get there.

Considering Adoption

After about four unsuccessful years of trying to have a baby, we considered adoption and went to a meeting to investigate the possibility of beginning this long process. We fit all of the criteria except for one key one. The problem was that we were told that we needed to have given up trying to conceive naturally ourselves and have a letter from a doctor confirming this. We had not been told that it would never be possible for us to have a baby and we thought that my endometriosis was gone for good. After all, I am just sub-fertile, not infertile (I hate these labels by the way). We still thought we could have a baby of our own but wanted to start the adoption process just in case; if we got two babies – bonus!

We know that we would have loved an adopted child totally and utterly. Even if we had children of our own, they would not have been made to feel any different. Anyone who knows us knows that, but, of course, the system has to protect the children in its care and so that is the way it is. For ages, I could not even bear to watch advertisements on television for charities looking for donations to help starving or abused children because I longed to look after them and it seemed so unfair that we were not being given the chance to do so. To add insult to injury, magazines are full of stories of celebrities who seem to be able to adopt at the drop of a hat! It seemed very unjust but you have to understand the reasoning behind these rules and play the cards you are dealt. I actually toyed with the idea of wishing that there was something wrong which made it impossible for me to conceive so that at least we could have a baby through adoption. Of course, I didn't actually go that far because I was still hopeful that I would find a way to carry a pregnancy to full term.

Adoption is a wonderful option for couples who can't have their own children. I believe that it would be a privilege and a gift to give a loving home to a little soul who needs it. However, it is a long process (up to five years) and so our experience makes me all the more convinced that it is vital for couples to get to the root of their problems as quickly as possible so that no time is wasted in beginning this process.

The first step is to contact the adoption service in your local HSE office and the staff there will advise you when the next adoption meeting, for which you can register, will be held. This meeting will go through all of the steps you need to take and the staff will walk you through the adoption process. Even if you are adopting from abroad, you must go through your local HSE office so that, if you are eligible, you can attain what is called a 'passport to adopt'. This document will prove that you have met all of the legal requirements and security checks. You must fit the following criteria in order to be eligible to adopt a child:

- You both must be over 21 years of age (there are no upper age limits legally but most agencies apply their own).
- You must be married and living together.
- If you are a married person adopting alone, you must be legally separated from your spouse or they must have abandoned you.
- A widow or widower can adopt.
- You can adopt if you are a relative of the child.

A sole applicant who does not fall into the above categories may only adopt if the Adoption Authority of Ireland is satisfied that, in the particular circumstances of the case, the adoption is desirable. Two unmarried persons cannot adopt jointly.

Be prepared for the length of time it takes and, instead of getting frustrated, I would suggest using this time to do all of the things you won't be able to do when you finally get to bring your baby home. Have lots of fun, do a course, travel – just use the time well and it will be no time at all before you are holding your baby in your arms.

Surrogacy

Surrogacy would appear to be a great solution for couples who have tried everything else in their quest to have a baby. It is an arrangement where a woman carries and delivers a child for another person. Unfortunately, in Ireland, there is no legislation in place to ensure the necessary regulation for legitimate agencies to be established to coordinate and manage this practice. We have looked into surrogacy in the past and, at that time, if we had used the help of a surrogate, even if she had carried a baby conceived by us, in the eyes of the law the woman who actually gave birth to the baby would have been the legal mother and I would have had to adopt the baby.

A Commission on Assisted Human Reproduction was set up in 2000 by Micheál Martin, who was Minister for Health and Children at the time; you can view and download the 2005 Report of the Commission from the Department of Health's website: www.dohc.ie/publications/cahr.html. It covers all areas of assisted reproduction and is interesting reading. Chapter 7 deals with surrogacy. Apart from the lack of legislation, there are moral issues surrounding the idea of paying for a baby and what price you would put on human life. The Commission was of the opinion that a surrogate should be paid 'reasonable and legitimate expenses' and no more, as otherwise under current legislation the necessary subsequent adoption of the baby would not be legal because the Adoption Act 1952 makes it illegal to make or receive any payment or other reward in consideration of adoption.

Of course, from my standpoint, I think that if it helps couples who desperately want a baby, what harm if the surrogate makes a profit from giving them this gift of life? It would only be fair to compensate a woman for going through pregnancy, and all the attendant physical and emotional changes, on your behalf. I think the concern of the Commission is that it does not want to create a market of women selling their bodies as surrogates in order to make money, rather than doing it as an altruistic gift – so this fear should also be acknowledged. There is no easy answer, and there are legitimate desires and fears on both sides of the equation that should be acknowledged. I fully understand that the issue of human life is one that should be considered precious and given due consideration, but, of course, my point of view is that of someone who wishes that this legislation had been passed a long time ago as it may have provided a solution for us.

However, there is light at the end of the tunnel thanks to a High Court ruling in March 2013 in which a couple who had twins through a surrogate successfully argued for their right to be identified as the children's parents. In this case, the woman's sister gave birth to the twins and both parties consented to having the genetic mother recognised as the mother on the birth certificate. The couple argued that the State-endorsed practice of using DNA tests to establish fatherhood conflicts with its stance that surrogate birth mothers are named legally as the child's mother. The High Court accepted their argument and ruled that the genetic parents would be recognised as the legal parents. It appears that legislation should be brought in by the end of 2013, which will make further recommendations with regard to surrogacy.

It makes me very emotional to think about the four women in my life who have offered to act as a surrogate for us on several occasions. It is a huge thing to offer to do for someone and I am so grateful for the fact that these amazing women care about us so much. Despite this, knowing myself as I do, I always declined their unbelievably kind offers. These women are kind and strong and I never doubted their confidence that they would be able to hand the baby they had carried for us for nine months over to our care, especially as the plan would be that it would be our baby that they would be carrying. However, I always believed that because I am so close to them it is more complicated than that single moment in the hospital. I had several worries. First of all, if there was a miscarriage, I was concerned that it would really hard on them physically. They would be very upset emotionally and possibly feel guilty. There were other people in their lives who would also be affected by the arrangement. I could not risk even the chance that seeing the baby grow up might be hard for them in the future. To be completely honest, part of me was also scared that they would be totally fed up of me by the end of the pregnancy because I would have been a total pain in the neck about diet, and so on. My concerns were all based on the fact that I had been through so much and thought I knew what all of the possible pitfalls would feel like. However, private surrogacy arrangements can also work very well. I think that you have to know yourself well and decide what would work for you personally.

Until recently, surrogacy was not discussed much. I did not know of anyone I could talk to for whom it had worked well and from whom I could get advice. I believed that without legislation, it is an area fraught with possible disappointments and difficulties.

I think that a 'professional' surrogate, working through an agency, would be a great solution for many couples. Naturally, the surrogate mother would have to be psychologically assessed and not suffer any emotional harm from taking part in the arrangement. However, it works in other countries and surely it is worth studying surrogate mothers' experiences in, for example, the United States. The Commission reported that children born through surrogacy are cared for exceptionally well so how can it be a bad thing?

In January 2013 the Minister for Health stated that legislation was being drafted, but there is no more recent news. Several articles in the wake of the recent High Court surrogacy case have called for legislation and for the Commission's now eight-year-old recommendations to be implemented. We can only hope that this will soon be done.

Pomegranate.ie (Financial Help for Couples Who Need IVF)

Pomegranate is a wonderful charity that was set up by two women to help fund couples who really want to have a baby, need IVF and cannot afford to pay for private treatment. Couples applying to the charity to help fund their IVF treatment must both hold medical cards. As Pomegranate is a relatively new and small charity, it obviously cannot help everyone who applies so it selects recipient couples via a lottery system.

My sister and I are hoping to help this charity through our business. If you want to learn more or make a donation (anything at all) the website is www.pomegranate.ie. You could be helping a couple fulfil their dream of having a family. It would be a great idea to 'like' Pomegranate on Facebook and find out how you could help with fundraising. After all, as more people become aware of this charity and more funds are raised, more couples will be helped.

Let's Hear It for the Boys

When I thought about writing this book, I asked Dessie if he wanted to write a chapter from the man's point of view. He declined and he definitely would not want me to write anything on his behalf. However, I feel the need to very generally point out that men do not often have anyone to talk to about the problems they face in dealing with fertility issues. Nobody brings them out for a pint to ask how they are coping and offer to let them vent. When they are as kind as my husband, they don't want to let their partners know how badly they feel for fear of making us feel worse. They also have to deal with situations where they feel left out of conversations and have no funny stories about their kids, or photos to pass around of their little treasures. I cannot imagine that most men would want to have hugely in-depth conversations about what is going on but I am sure that it would be gratifying for someone to acknowledge what they must be going through and to ask if they can help and just let them know that they can talk to them if they need to. Let's face it – they have to comfort us when we cry, deal with their own disappointment, help us with injections, sit in hospitals waiting for us to come out of surgery and nurse us back to normality after miscarriages, while worrying if they will ever get back the woman they love. Our knights in shining armour deserve at least a standing ovation and our endless love.

Optimism and Positivity

I am a glass-half-full kind of girl. This has resulted in me being absolutely positive every month for the last eight years that this was the month and whatever treatment or therapy I was trying out was 'the one'. Obviously, as I don't have a houseful of children, I was terribly wrong! Sometimes, I have wondered if my optimism stopped me from being more demanding and insistent. If I had been more freaked out, if I had made a fuss á la Veruca Salt in *Charlie and the Chocolate Factory*, would someone have done something different to ensure I had my baby more quickly? However, I have come to the conclusion that my optimism kept me sane. While it doesn't guarantee immediate success, if you are optimistic and positive about the future you are enjoying today and that is all we have – today and now! Not all personalities are the same and not all people are naturally optimistic, but by cultivating a positive outlook on life it can be easier to deal with disappointments and heartache.

5

How to Help a Friend with Fertility Issues

Due to the rising statistics of couples facing fertility challenges, it is very likely that we all know someone going through this difficult time. I know how upsetting it feels to know that you are making someone else feel awkward and how it has added to my distress in the past. Some people believe that perhaps it is not polite to bring up difficult subjects. The definition of politeness in our family has always been that you make sure everyone in your company is comfortable. While it would not be polite to bring up infertility in a crowd, when you are talking one-to-one with your friend it is polite to consider how she is and let her know that she has the space to talk about whatever is going on with her. You should never worry that it might make her cry because if she does, then she needed to. Crying is a great release of emotion. I am brilliant at it, but thankfully equally enjoy laughing. I am hoping that this chapter will help to guide people in certain circumstances so that this taboo or awkwardness can be eliminated once and for all. You could also read Chapter 4 to gain some comprehension of what your friend is going through. If you are generous enough to want to understand what your friend is going through and to want to know how to help her, then you are a good friend already.

Do I Ask Her About Her Problems?

If you are her friend, of course you do. How else will she know that you care about her? Obviously you should have this conversation in an appropriate place. I remember a friend of mine tried to convince me that I needed IVF in a coffee shop one time and I was mortified. First of all, because she hadn't listened to what my problems were and IVF was possibly not my immediate solution and, secondly, because I didn't want to talk about it *there*. It wasn't long after a miscarriage and I was still fairly hormonal and afraid I was going to burst out crying. However, even though I closed up and wouldn't talk to her about it that day, thankfully she persisted and has been a great friend throughout this time. A couple of other friends, with and without children, have been great too. They ask me how things are in a normal voice and as part of a normal conversation and don't make me feel like a freak or like they are walking on eggshells around me. If I mention that I have an occasion to go to that they think might be hard for me, such as a Christening or a child's birthday party, they will say 'Oh crikey, bet you can't wait for that', and this makes me laugh. While some occasions have been hard, depending on what is going on for us at the time, I don't actually mind occasions with babies and children because I love them. Anyway, I feel it's worse to be left out. But I love that my friends make me feel that if I didn't want to go it would be natural and not make me a bad person. However, I also have some friends who have never asked me anything about my problems, even though I have referred to it in an attempt to communicate what I am going through. What I have had to remind myself is that it doesn't mean that they don't care; they just don't know what to say and that is ok because they let me know they are thinking about us in other ways. However, for those of you who want to find a way to talk to your friend about her situation, know that just acknowledging what she is going through will help her enormously and give her strength.

I watched a programme on television called *Beatles Stories* recently, in which people from all walks of life who had come into contact with The Beatles told their anecdotes. One of them was a concert promoter for the Hollywood Bowl. On the day of The Beatles' concert, there were thousands more people trying to get tickets than were available. He was being pressurised by celebrities and friends, not to mention the tens of thousands of fans hanging around outside the venue. He was having a bad day and then he was summoned to The Beatles' dressing room. Paul McCartney said that he heard he was having a tough time and he should let them know if there was anything that they or any of their team could do to help. There wasn't much that they could do as the venue was only so big but the promoter felt instantly better and he said that the validation from Sir Paul (as he is now) made him feel that he would go to the ends of the earth for him. That statement struck a chord with me and that is how I feel about the many people who have supported and, to use his word, validated me on my bad days.

How Do I Help Her When She Has Had a Miscarriage?

You must realise that although no one else has seen or known this baby, your friend is experiencing profound grief and feels as though she has actually lost a part of herself. Initially, she will be in shock and not even know how she feels herself. Text as soon as you hear because while she might not feel like talking, she will appreciate being reminded that you care about her. One of my friends told me recently that while she had been texting me when I was in hospital with my last miscarriage, she had felt that her texts were useless and was frustrated that she did not seem to have the right words to say. One of her texts said that she was hoping the procedure went as well as it could and she said that she had thought twice about sending it because the procedure was a D&C and all that that entails. I was really glad to have the opportunity to let her know that all of the texts that we received in hospital meant a lot to both Dessie and me. It wasn't the words that mattered. It was truly the thought that counted and I was so glad she sent that text.

Give her a few days to get over the worst of the shock and then call out to see her. Just be with her and listen to her when she is ready to talk. Don't be afraid of saying 'I am sorry for your loss', like you would at any other funeral. You don't have to understand, just listen. Do not try to make her feel better by suggesting that she can try again because it is too soon. She needs to grieve for this baby, this little person for whom she had already made so many plans and whose little face she desperately wanted to see and know. This pain does not go away overnight and the following few months can be difficult so don't expect her to get back to herself straight away. She will be angry for a while and then perhaps desperately obsessed with conceiving again before what would have been her due date. Try to remember her due date and make sure you mention it to her and check in with her to see if she is ok. Maybe organise a get-together around that time with a group of friends to make her feel supported. It will be more difficult if she has not conceived again by that time so just give her the space to feel whatever she needs to feel and let her know that you are there to listen whenever she needs it.

How Do I Tell Her that I Am Pregnant?

Congratulations! You have just learned that you are pregnant and it is wonderful news. Once you get over the initial excitement and you and your partner are starting to think about telling people, it occurs to you that your news may be hard for someone really close to you or in your immediate circle, if she has just had a miscarriage or has been through a number of miscarriages. You are feeling awkward and don't want to upset her. Please don't chicken out because how you handle this will make a difference to your relationship as it speaks bucket-loads about how you feel about your friend. If you are respectful and kind, you will make it so much easier on her and earn yourself a friend for life. Here's what to do:

- Don't go around telling everyone else how much you are dreading telling her – this is completely disrespectful.
- Forget about texting, phoning or getting someone else to do it. Call out to her home and tell her over a cup of tea in the privacy of her own kitchen. It doesn't matter if you are awkward and blub a bit – she will see that it is because you care about her and that is what matters.
- Tell her that you wish it was her too and that she deserves it as much as you.
- She will be delighted for you but if you spot that she is upset, be her shoulder to cry on and if you feel like it, cry with her.
- Tell her a few days before everyone else in your circle to give her a chance to get her happy face on once everyone starts saying what wonderful news it is (which of course every pregnancy is).

- Be sensitive to when you feel she might want you to leave if she wants to have a little cry by herself.
- Remember that any upset she might feel has nothing to do with how happy she is for you.

Of course, your pregnancy is all about you, and your friend would absolutely not want it to be all about her, but if you do this she will be in no doubt that you care about and respect what she is going through. In your bliss, it is not too much to ask to be a little generous with your time and emotions to help someone you care about, and this makes you a really good person.

How Do I Help Her Deal with My Pregnancy?

Watching someone close to you glowing during pregnancy is a wonderful thing but if you have suffered miscarriages or are having difficulty conceiving it can also be a form of torture. This is especially true if you conceived at the same time so every new stage of development is one that you should have been going through together. To top it off, there is also the dread of how you will feel when the baby is born and how on earth you will be able to hide your grief. If you are pregnant and aware that this may be the case for someone close to you, don't stay away from her or make her feel as though she is making you feel awkward. This only adds the feeling of abandonment to the list of stressful emotions she is going through. Ask her how things are going and what she is doing with regard to treatments or if she needs any help researching any options that may be available for her.

She will probably ask you polite questions about how you are doing, so tell her, but there is no need for too many details. For example, if you know that she has only ever had silent scans don't go on about how lovely it is to hear your baby's heartbeat. It may seem obvious, but you would be surprised how many people let their mouths run away with them when they are not thinking or are nervous. Try not to complain too much about tiredness and so on because she would gladly suffer tiredness, varicose veins and everything else if it meant she could have her own baby. Respect how strong she will have to be to watch this baby grow up, while grieving for her own loss. You would be surprised at how much easier you can make things for people by just acknowledging their situation and showing you actually care. For me, this positive approach has completely dissipated any upset I have felt and made me feel happy in the knowledge that I am cared for.

How Do I Help Her Deal with the Birth of My Baby?

It would be lovely if you discussed this with her before the baby comes. Tell her that you would love if she could come to meet your baby privately with no one else around. If it's in the hospital, ask her to come before visiting hours, for example. It will be so much easier for her knowing that there are not several pairs of eyes on her waiting to see how she is coping. Keep this between yourselves and, if anyone asks, say she is coping beautifully. Have respect for how strong she is. When you get home and while your baby still has that newborn look about them, if you want to call out to see her, make sure that other people are not there. For some reason, it was very hard for me having other people meet newborns in my own home at times when they should have been meeting my baby. I know that you will be busy with your little bundle of joy, and good for you. This is a wonderful time for you and you absolutely should enjoy every minute of it. Just because you feel badly for your friend because she lost her baby does not mean that you should not be happy for yourself. She is happy for you and relieved that your baby is well. She would not want a big fuss or be made to feel self-conscious or that she is taking anything from you. However, if you really love your friend, a little care will go a long way to ensuring she is a friend for life.

What If I Put My Foot In It?

Well of course you will, because you are human like me and everyone else. I acknowledge that it is very difficult because there are no exact rules about what you can or can't say because different things hurt on different days and you are not a mind reader. However, you have a mouth in your head and God gave it to you for a reason – *to use it*. When in doubt, ask. Two people could say exactly the same insensitive thing to me and hearing it from one would not bother me but hearing it from another could really hurt me. I realised that this is due to the 'consider the source' rule. If it was from someone I did not know very well, an acquaintance who didn't know anything about what I was dealing with, then I couldn't get upset by an offhand remark. However, if the remark came from someone who I thought cared about me and who I was close to and who should know that such a comment would hurt me in some way, then that is a different story. It became clear to me that what made me upset was not *what* they said but the fact that the person who I thought cared about me did not appear to consider my feelings at all. However, such hurt can be quickly dissipated with a simple acknowledge-ment that the comment was insensitive – 'Oh crikey, have I said something stupid? I didn't mean to make you feel bad, I'm sorry.' The situation is then forgotten about because care and respect have been shown. I try to use this theory when I put my foot in it – like I said, we're all human.

How Do I Help My Friend through Long-Term Fertility Challenges?

What you need to know is that while your life is moving along either with your own family or with your career, your friend can often feel as though she is in a limbo of doctors' appointments, fertility cycles, getting hopes up and then crushed and then the same again month after month, and that her life is not moving in any direction. There is no need to bring the subject up in every conversation, but every now and then you can just check in with her to see how she is. Listen and empathise – never pity. Tell her she would be a great mum but that she has so much going for her anyway outside of that. Tell her that you can see how strong she is and admire her. Throughout all of this, her self-confidence is taking a bashing as well.

Some people seem to react well to a drama. If something awful happens people rally around, but the true friends are the ones who are around on the 'limbo' days too. That is the thing about going through tough times, you really find out who your friends are. Don't try to tell your friend what she should do because if you haven't been there then, let's face it, you haven't a clue. By all means, tell her if you have seen something fertility related in the media, but don't tell her she should do X or Y and all her problems will be solved. What you do is you show interest in how she is feeling and handling things and what treatments she is considering. Just be supportive and send texts on days when she has procedures to let her know that you are thinking of her. Ask her what she needs from you if you don't know. Make her laugh! Support any decision she makes. If she decides to go to Timbuktu to try out an ancient remedy, then say 'Go for it!' If she decides that it is time to give up, tell her she is dead right. At the end of the day, she has to deal with it herself, but by being a friend you will make things a hundredfold easier.

Dessie and my family support me on my bad days in too many ways to list, from just listening and sometimes crying with me (girls only of course), to making me laugh, sending texts when I am in tough situations, giving me makeovers (Rachel) and feeding me (I admit I'm obsessed with food), but whatever they do it is the love behind it that makes me feel great and like I can cope. That is all you really need to know.

Conclusion

This is the book I wish I had at the beginning of our baby wait. It was important to me to write it before this particular chapter closed for me, so that you, the readers going through fertility challenges, can feel that I am relating to you. Even though I have been through a lot, I have kept an open heart and mind, and learned a lot from my experiences over the past nine years. I have now shared every little and big thing I have learned along the way with you so that this information can hopefully save some precious time and shorten your baby wait. It would be easy for me to bemoan the fact that I had to go through so much to get to this point but I choose to believe that the reason will become apparent in time. Actually, the best lesson that I have learned along the way is that whatever happens I am excited for the future. There are lots of experiences out there and I know that I am strong, happy and have the tools to cope with whatever new challenges life presents. I am not so busy worrying about outcomes that I miss the good things happening today. Life is always going to have its ups and downs but if you focus on and make the most of the good, you will endure the bad and be stronger for it.

So, I shall sign off now and I can't tell you how much I hope something in this book has helped you. Remember one thing – life is short. So find your joy as much as you can, no matter what cards you are dealt. As the great Stephen Covey taught us, 'Live, learn, love and leave a legacy.'

Wishing you health and happiness,
Luv Lyn xxx

Glossary

The following are a list of terms that you should know as they relate directly to your fertility:

Cervical mucus: The glands in the cervix produce cervical mucus when stimulated by the presence of oestrogen. This is very important for conception as it protects the sperm, keeps it alive for up to five days in the womb and helps to transport it towards the fallopian tube, thereby helping conception.

Corpus luteum: This is what is left of the follicle after ovulation. It produces progesterone which thickens the lining of the womb for implantation and is necessary to sustain a healthy pregnancy. It continues to produce progesterone until the placenta takes over at about ten weeks into your pregnancy.

D&C: Dilation and curettage – a gynaecological procedure sometimes used after a miscarriage to remove the foetus from the uterus.

Endometrium: The lining of the uterus, which thickens during the first half of your menstrual cycle in anticipation of implantation by a fertilised egg. If fertilisation does not occur, the endometrium will break down and exit the body as a menstrual period.

Fallopian tube: The fallopian tubes are two tubes that connect to a woman's uterus (one on each side). The other ends of the tubes flare open with several long fringes, called fimbrae, on the end. After ovulation, these fimbrae beat back and forth to help guide the egg into the fallopian tube. Once inside the tube, tiny hairs called cilia push the egg along and toward the uterus. Fertilisation typically occurs in the fallopian tube if the egg encounters a sperm.

Follicle: A follicle is like a balloon which is filled with fluid and contains an egg. Each ovary contains many follicles, each of which holds an immature ovum or egg.

Follicle-stimulating hormone: FSH is released by the anterior pituitary gland in the brain and is present in both men and women. In women, it stimulates the follicles in our ovaries to ripen several eggs (although generally only one will mature) and to produce oestradiol during the first half of our cycle. FSH also readies the mammary glands for milk production.

In men, this hormone stimulates the production of sperm. This can be tested with a blood sample. To test levels in women, the blood sample will have to be taken on certain days of the month.

Hormone: A hormone is chemical substance which travels through the bloodstream to regulate the activity of certain organs. Hormones are produced by organs, glands or special cells. This is why your overall general health is so important to your fertility, because hormones are the basis of your fertility and when something is unbalanced elsewhere in the body, your fertility is naturally affected.

ICSI: Intracytoplasmic sperm injection is a form of IVF where a single sperm is injected directly into the egg.

IUI: Intrauterine insemination is a treatment in which the best quality sperm is placed in the uterus during a medical procedure to improve the chances of fertilisation.

IVF: In vitro fertilisation is a process in which an egg is fertilised by sperm outside the body, in a laboratory, and the fertilised egg is then transferred into the uterus.

Laparoscopy: A keyhole procedure where a small camera is used to inspect the uterus, ovaries and fallopian tubes.

Luteal phase: The length of time from ovulation to menstruation. This should be approximately fourteen days. If it is too short, this could indicate low progesterone levels.

Luteinizing hormone: LH is another hormone released by the pituitary gland in the brain. The increase of this hormone in women causes ovulation to occur, i.e. the release of the egg from the follicles. The secretion of LH also signals the remnants of the follicles to develop into the corpus luteum. LH is also produced by men, in whom it stimulates the production of testosterone. Levels of LH are tested with a blood sample. Mid-stream (urine) ovulation tests can also be used to test for a surge in LH.

Oestrogen: Oestrogen is a hormone whose main function is to promote the development and maintenance of female reproductive organs. This includes the fat distribution to all those curvy bits that make us female. It also maintains the health of our inner reproductive organs, especially the endometrial lining of the uterus. Oestrogen prepares the follicle for the release of an egg, controls the change in our cervical mucus and makes sure our wombs are sperm friendly. It also helps to maintain our bone density by increasing bone-forming cells and assists in the maintenance of fluid and electrolyte balance within our bodies. There are three main types of oestrogen produced by our bodies: oestrodial, which is secreted by the ovaries; oestrone, which is produced by the adrenal glands (this is more important post menopause); and oestriol, which is made primarily in the liver, and is a by-product of the first two.

Ovary: The female reproductive organ in which eggs are produced.

Ovulation: A woman's ovaries contain tiny fluid-filled follicles. As the egg grows the follicle builds up fluid. When the egg matures, the follicle breaks open and the egg is released and travels through the fallopian tube towards the uterus. This is called ovulation.

Ovum: A mature egg that is ready for fertilisation.

Progesterone: Progesterone is the hormone of development. It is produced in the corpus luteum and also lesser quantities are produced in the adrenal glands. It works with oestrogen in preparing the womb for possible pregnancy. It stimulates the lining of the fallopian tubes so they provide nutrition for the ovum as it travels to the uterus for implantation. Increased levels of progesterone after ovulation cause enlarged and sore breasts before your period. This enlargement happens so that the breasts are prepared for milk production, but it is prolactin which actually causes the milk production. Progesterone can stimulate your appetite and it also has an effect on the kidneys which causes them to store more salt and water. This is why women can bloat and feel heavier in the second half of their cycle. It can also cause PMS symptoms. Post ovulation, progesterone also makes cervical mucus thicker, which acts like a natural plug for the cervix, thus protecting the possible baby. It also improves fat metabolism, increases bone density, elevates your mood and helps prevent cancerous and benign breast and uterine changes.

Prolactin: This hormone is released by the pituitary gland to stimulate breast development and the production of milk in women.

Sperm: Sperm derives from a Greek word meaning seed and refers to the male reproductive cells.

Testes: The pair of male reproductive glands contained within the scrotum, whose function is to produce sperm.

Thyroid: The thyroid is one of the largest endocrine glands, located in the throat. It produces a number of hormones and also plays an important role in regulating your metabolism and controlling your body's sensitivity to a wide range of hormones. It is really important that your thyroid gland is functioning normally, i.e. it is not over-active or underactive.

An underactive thyroid (hypothyroidism) increases the risk of miscarriage, premature birth, gestational hypertension and pre-eclampsia, as well as slow intellectual development in children. Hypothyroidism leads to irregular ovulation and increasing production of prolactin which causes the production of immature eggs.

An overactive thyroid (hyperthyroidism) can pose special concerns during pregnancy. When the body delivers too much thyroid hormone both mother and baby can suffer. Miscarriages and premature births can occur when the disorder goes undiagnosed or untreated. Pregnant women with hyperthyroidism can also develop high blood pressure and are at greater risk of heart conditions. Hyperthyroidism causes low levels of oestrogen which cannot trigger the production of LH, which stimulates ovulation, thus leading to infertility.

Ultrasound: An ultrasound is a high frequency sound that humans cannot hear, but it can be emitted and detected by special machines. An ultrasound test is a painless test which is carried out to examine a particular area of the body. In the case of fertility or pregnancy tests, we are talking about the pelvic area. There are two types. The first is where a lubricating gel is spread across your tummy and the probe (like a big blunt pen) is passed across and this sends pictures of your womb to a monitor. The second is where the probe, covered with a condom and gel, is inserted into the vagina and this can give a clearer picture of your womb and reproductive organs. Ultrasounds are carried out to check on your baby's progress and health and also provide information to doctors if you are having difficulty in conceiving.

Uterus: The organ in which a growing foetus develops after a fertilised egg is implanted in the endometrium. Also called the womb.

Recommended Reading

Mike Adams, *Superfoods for Optimum Health: Chlorella and Spirulina* (Truth Publishing, 2009).

Alan E. Beer, *Is Your Body Baby-Friendly?* (AJR Publishing LLC, 2006).

Peter Boylan, *The Irish Pregnancy Book: A Guide for Expectant Mothers* (A & A Farmar, 2005).

Gloria Chacon de Popovici, *Maca: Millenarian Peruvian Food Plant, with Highly Nutritional and Medicinal Values* (translated from Spanish into English) (Lima, 2001).

Stephen Covey, *The 7 Habits of Highly Effective People* (Simon & Schuster, 2004).

Marilyn Glenville, *Getting Pregnant Faster: Boost Your Fertility in just 3 Months – Naturally* (Kyle Cathie Limited, 2008).

Patrick Holford, *Optimum Nutrition Before, During and After Pregnancy* (Piatkus, 2009).

Beth M. Lacey, *Maca: Native Food and Medicine of Peru – Adaptogen and Hormonal Regulator* (A Healthy Alternative LLC, 2003).

Jan Lovejoy, *Get Balanced: The Natural Way to Better Health with Superfoods* (SGN Nutrition LLC, 2007).

Dermot O'Connor, *The Healing Code: One Man's Amazing Journey Back to Health and His Proven Five-Step Plan to Recovery* (Hachette Ireland, 2007).

Patrick Quillan, *Beating Cancer with Nutrition* (Nutrition Times Press, 2005).

Walter Shantree Kacera, *Ayurvedic Tongue Diagnosis* (Lotus Press, 2006).

Mark Stengler, *The Natural Physician's Healing Therapies* (Prentice Hall Press, 2010).

Thompson Healthcare Inc, *PDR for Herbal Medicines*, fourth edition (Thomson Reuters, 2007).

Toni Weschler, *Taking Charge of Your Fertility: The Definitive Guide to Natural Birth Control, Pregnancy Achievement, and Reproductive Health*, tenth anniversary edition (MPH Harper Collins Publishers, 2006).

Zita West, *Zita West's Guide to Getting Pregnant: The Complete Programme from the Renowned Fertility Expert* (Thorsons Publishers, 2005).

Useful Websites

Pregnancy, Fertility and Menstruation

Baby Center:	www.babycenter.com
Menstruation.com.au:	www.menstruation.com.au
American Pregnancy Association:	www.americanpregnancy.org
WomensHealth.gov:	www.womenshealth.gov
Is Your Body Baby-Friendly?:	www.babyfriendlybook.com
About.com Infertility:	www.infertility.about.com

Information Databases

WebMD:	www.webmd.com
MedlinePlus:	www.nlm.nih.gov/medlineplus
National Center for Biotechnology Information:	www.ncbi.nlm.nih.gov
Ezine Articles:	www.ezinearticles.com
About.com:	www.about.com

Health

Caffeine during pregnancy:	www.babycenter.com/caffeine-during-pregnancy
Smoking during pregnancy:	www.babycenter.com/0_how-smoking-during-pregnancy-affects-you-and-your-baby_1405720.bc

en.wikipedia.org/wiki/
    Smoking_and_pregnancy

Alcohol Action Ireland:	alcoholireland.ie
Diabetes Ireland:	www.diabetes.ie
Pregnancy and diabetes:	www.diabetes.ie/
	living-with-diabetes/
	pregnancy-and-diabetes
Diabetes:	www.nlm.nih.gov/medlineplus/
	ency/article/001214.htm
Asthma Society of Ireland:	www.asthmasociety.ie
Positive Nutrition:	positivenutrition.ie

Superfoods and Supplements

Açaí berry:	www.acaiberry.org
Chlorella:	www.chlorellafactor.com
Maca root:	www.macaperu.com
Clinical studies of maca root:	www.ahealthya.com/Scientific_
	Study.htm
	www.macaperu.com/Clinical%20
	Trials%20For%20Gelati-
	nized%20Maca.htm
Supplemental Science:	www.supplementalscience.com
Ireland's Raw Kitchen:	www.irelandsrawkitchen.ie
Andean Harvest:	www.andeanharvest.com
The Happy Pear:	www.thehappypear.ie
WH Foods:	www.whfoods.com
Body Ecology:	www.bodyecology.com
Synergy Natural:	www.synergynatural.com

Tests

Maybe Baby saliva testing:	www.maybebabyovulation.com
Antral follicle count:	www.advancedfertility.com/
	antralfollicles.htm
AMH blood test:	www.advancedfertility.com/
	amh-fertility-test.htm

Chromosome analysis:	atlantichealth.dnadirect.com/ grc/patient-site/chromo- some-analysis-infertility/ chromosome-analysis-and- fertility.html
Thyroid function test:	www.nlm.nih.gov/medlineplus/ ency/article/003444.htm
Prolactin blood test:	www.nlm.nih.gov/medlineplus/ ency/article/003718.htm
LH blood test:	www.nlm.nih.gov/medlineplus/ ency/article/003708.htm
FSH blood test:	www.nlm.nih.gov/medlineplus/ ency/article/003710.htm
Glucose blood test:	www.nlm.nih.gov/medlineplus/ ency/article/003482.htm
Pelvic laparoscopy:	www.nlm.nih.gov/medlineplus/ ency/article/002916.htm
Cambridge Nutritional Sciences Ltd:	www.camnutri.com

Treatments

IVF:	www.ivf-infertility.com www.infertility.about.com/ od/infertilitytreatments/ss/ ivf_treatment_2.htm
IUI:	www.repromed.ie/iui/
ICSI:	www.sims.ie/Home/ Intracytoplasmic_Sperm_Injec- tion_ICSI.1040.html

Fertility Treatment Centres

ReproMed:	www.repromed.ie
Mayo Clinic:	www.mayoclinic.com
The Fertility Institutes:	www.fertility-docs.com
Shared Journey:	www.sharedjourney.com

Advanced Fertility Center of
   Chicago: www.advancedfertility.com

Natural Treatments

NaPro Technology: www.fertilitycare.ie
EZ Fertility: www.ez-fertility.co.uk
                                  www.itsnatural.com.au
Natural Fertility Info: www.natural-fertility-info.com

Complementary Therapies

Acupuncture: www.medicalacupuncture.org
Reflexology: www.reflexologist.ie
Craniosacral therapy: www.craniosacral-therapy-
                                     healing.com
                                  www.clearpassage.com/infertility
                                  www.nestlondon.com
Maya womb massage: www.fertilehands.com
                                  www.mayatherapy.ie
Emotional freedom techniques: www.emofree.com
Salt therapy: asthmasociety.ie/
                                     asthma-information/
                                     speleotherapysalt-cave-therapy-
                                     as-a-complementary-treatment-
                                     for-asthma
                                  www.salttherapyireland.com

Common Medical Problems

Ectopic pregnancy: www.webmd.com/baby/tc/
                                     ectopic-pregnancy-topic-over-
                                     view
Molar pregnancy: www.molarpregnancy.co.uk
Uterine fibroids: www.mayoclinic.com/health/
                                     uterine-fibroids/DS00078

Polycystic ovary syndrome:	www.pcosinireland.com
	pcosireland.ning.com
Endometriosis:	www.endometriosis.co.uk
Asherman syndrome:	www.ashermans.org
Yeast infections:	natural-fertility-info.com/
	candida-fertility.html
Cushing syndrome:	www.cushings-help.com
Sperm health:	www.mayoclinic.com/health/
	fertility/MC00023
Retrograde ejaculation	www.webmd.com/infertility-
	and-reproduction/guide/
	retrograde-ejaculation
Varicoceles:	varicoceles.com/
	what-is-a-varicocele
Epididymal obstruction:	www.wernermd.com/
	obstruction.php
Male bacterial infections:	www.livestrong.com/
	article/82547-male-infertility-
	bacterial-infections

Support Groups and Organisations

Miscarriage Association of Ireland:	www.miscarriage.ie
Miscarriage Association (UK):	www.miscarriageassociation.org. uk
National Infertility Support and Information Group:	www.nisig.ie
Pomegranate:	www.pomegranate.ie

Miscellaneous

Adoption Authority of Ireland:	www.aai.gov.ie
Report of the Commission on Assisted Human Reproduction:	www.dohc.ie/publications/cahr. html
Money Advice & Budgeting Service:	www.mabs.ie

Temple Street Children's University Hospital: www.cuh.ie

Our Lady's Children's Hospital, Crumlin: www.olchc.ie